FROM PROBLEM SOLVING TO SOLUTION DESIGN

J. EDUARDO CAMPOS & ERICA W. CAMPOS

FROM
PROBLEM SOLVING
TO
SOLUTION DESIGN

TURNING IDEAS INTO ACTIONS

ForbesBooks

Published by ForbesBooks, Charleston, South Carolina.
Member of Advantage Media Group.

ForbesBooks is a registered trademark, and the ForbesBooks colophon is a trademark of Forbes Media, LLC.

Printed in the United States of America.

10 9 8 7 6 5 4 3 2 1

ISBN: 978-0-998365-56-5
LCCN: 2018934787

Cover design by Melanie Cloth.
Layout design by Megan Elger.

This publication is designed to provide accurate and authoritative information in regard to the subject matter covered. It is sold with the understanding that the publisher is not engaged in rendering legal, accounting, or other professional services. If legal advice or other expert assistance is required, the services of a competent professional person should be sought.

Advantage Media Group is proud to be a part of the Tree Neutral® program. Tree Neutral offsets the number of trees consumed in the production and printing of this book by taking proactive steps such as planting trees in direct proportion to the number of trees used to print books. To learn more about Tree Neutral, please visit **www.treeneutral.com**.

Since 1917, the Forbes mission has remained constant. Global Champions of Entrepreneurial Capitalism. ForbesBooks exists to further that aim by bringing the Stories, Passion, and Knowledge of top thought leaders to the forefront. ForbesBooks brings you The Best in Business. To be considered for publication, please visit **www.forbesbooks.com**.

To our families, who taught us by example that giving first is the best way to receive, who have selflessly offered us their endless love, and who have generously invested their time and resources to allow us to become who we are and to get where we are today.

TABLE OF CONTENTS

NEW TIMES–NEW CHALLENGES

IDENTIFY *Define the Essential Problem and Prioritize Your Actions to Solve the Essential Problem*

DESIGN *Set Your Goals for the Solution Design and Design Solution Options*

ENGAGE *Prepare Your Stakeholder Engagement Plan and Influence the Decision-Making Process*

ACT *Drive Your Implementation Strategy and Execute Your Governance Model*

SUSTAIN *Leverage the Organizational Lifecycle and Create a Feedback Loop*

ACKNOWLEDGMENTS -------------

We want to acknowledge the invaluable guidance, help, and support we have received from several people that allowed us to realize our dream of writing this—our first book—hopefully paving the way for many to come.

Our families, who supported us from the beginning, were there for us from our "a-ha" moment in graduate school that sparked the crazy idea of writing a book throughout the writing process to the book's completion.

Our friends, who have shared our seemingly impossible dreams. They gave us invaluable feedback, and endured our absence while we were away writing this book.

Our professors, who were patient in sharing their knowledge. They encouraged us to always question the status quo, and went beyond teaching to prepare us for life.

Our clients and stakeholders, who trusted us when sharing their organizational complex problems. They believed in our commitment to help them create sustainable solutions and provided us with unique insights and candid feedback, allowing us to grow professionally and individually.

Our managers, from whom we have learned the difference between being a leader and acting as a real one.

Our teams and peers, whose unconditional support and generous feedback helped us correct the course and improve our Solution-Design process through continuous learning.

Other authors, some of whom are cited in this book, who inspired us with their ingenuity, their kindness in sharing their knowledge, and their ability to communicate their ideas.

Our publishing team from Advantage Media Group | ForbesBooks, who were gracious in patiently responding to our endless questions. They guided us and cheered us along the way, from the beginning to the end of the book writing process.

ABOUT THE AUTHORS ------------

J. EDUARDO CAMPOS, EMPA
Author | Speaker | Solution Designer | Advisor

J. Eduardo is a seasoned strategist who designs sustainable solutions by building bridges across diverse groups.

After creating business growth opportunities on four continents through his leadership roles at PwC, Embraer, and Bell Canada, he spent thirteen years at Microsoft, first as a cybersecurity advisor, then leading innovative Microsoft projects at the highest levels of government in the US and abroad.

Today, J. Eduardo is realizing his dream of building a better tomorrow by leading his consulting firm, Embedded Knowledge, Inc., to develop value propositions, customize business strategies, and form partnerships that enable organizations and entrepreneurs to design creative solutions for their complex problems.

At Central Washington University (CWU), J. Eduardo is continually inspired by a talented group of people involved in Game On!, a program that inspires and empowers high school students in rural

Washington to attend college. There, purpose-driven professionals who work for Microsoft, the Real Madrid Foundation, and CWU enable young people who participate in the program (www.cwu.edu/game-on).

ERICA W. CAMPOS
Author | Speaker | Solution Designer | Advisor

Erica is seasoned compliance professional who is passionate about using her skills to build transparent, ethical, and sustainable relationships across diverse groups.

Currently a Compliance senior lead for Microsoft, Erica leverages her twenty-five-plus years in global management roles in large corporations in the financial (ABN Amro Banco Real) and consulting (PwC) industries.

Applying her agile collaboration, influencing, and negotiation skills to support the interests of all stakeholders, Erica has a solid record of designing solutions that mutually benefit all involved.

Enjoying life in the beautiful Pacific Northwest, J. Eduardo and Erica are strengthening their personal and professional partnership by opening a new chapter in their lives, which they term, "The Big Leap." It's the start of realizing their long-held dream to share their skills and passion for sparking innovation and building bridges between people, processes, and possibilities. They are confident that their Big Leap will achieve Big Impact for large audiences across the public and private sectors.

In their new book, *From Problem Solving to Solution Design: Turning Ideas into Actions*, rich with fresh ideas, approaches, and case studies, J. Eduardo and Erica offer their combined expertise—best practices they have gleaned and consolidated from their years of working in intercultural corporate environments—to help anyone in any organization of any size facing complex problems to formulate sustainable solutions for optimal outcomes.

As advisory board members of the University of Washington's Evans School of Public Policy and Governance, where they both got their executive master's degrees, they give back to the community that welcomed them with open arms by sharing the skills acquired from their journey.

FOREWORD --

NEW TIMES—NEW
CHALLENGES

After a professional career of forty-seven years as an aeronautical engineer at Boeing for Iberia Airlines of Spain, and having served as the Honorary Consul of Spain for twenty-three years in the states of Washington and Oregon, I saw first-hand the global transformation that the airline industry underwent in the 1970s. The first wave of globalization made the populations of five continents much more accessible to one another. Living in Seattle, I bore witness to the transformations that a small number of entrepreneurs initiated in the 1980s, which gave us the tools to communicate and access information instantaneously. This changed the business world as we knew it, and altered the way we conducted business. Among the corporations that originated in Seattle and have had a profound effect on how we live, communicate, and consume products are Microsoft, Amazon, Nordstrom, Boeing, Costco, Expedia, T-Mobile, AT&T Wireless, Sprint, Paccar, and Starbucks.

I have tried to discern how one city generated an entrepreneurial revolution in such singular way—ultimately affecting the entire world, changing our lives, and the way we all create and run our businesses. The only explanation I have found is that there was a small group of visionaries who created an ecosystem of entrepreneurs and philanthropists around a great public university—the University of Washington. The University of Washington is ranked tenth in the *US News and World Report's* 2018 Best Global University rankings—tied with Johns Hopkins University and Yale University—and has transformed Seattle—a city which in July 1971 displayed a billboard on the freeway that read, "Will the last person leaving Seattle please turn out the lights?"—into the fastest urban growth center in the United States.[1]

Within just a few years we have seen our entrepreneurial world completely transform. In the past, decisions were made based on instinct, limited information, years of experience, personal credibility, and personal communication skills, involving only a few people in the daily decision-making.

Today, everything has changed with the networking capabilities of computers, mobile telephones, and big data, which have put all available information in the hands of all those involved in the chain of decision-making, allowing them to communicate instantaneously and without even meeting or seeing one another. Human contact has all

---

1   Best Global Universities Rankings," *US News and World Report*, (2018): https://www.usnews.com/education/best-global-universities/rankings?page=2.

but disappeared, which has changed the way in which we work as well as the way we recognize, analyze, and look for resolutions to problems.

J. Eduardo Campos and Erica W. Campos have taken these changes, and with their vast entrepreneurial experience in this new business environment, incorporated the concepts into an excellent new book, *From Problem Solving to Solution-Design: Turning Ideas into Actions.*

I have had the opportunity to work with J. Eduardo in the last five years, first in his role as the Worldwide Director of Business Development at Microsoft, managing the team leading over one hundred Microsoft Innovation Centers. He has impressed me with his vision and his ability to detect problems and create solutions. He involves everyone by creating a team in which all members have the same goal: to look for a solution that is sustainable and scalable, because if it is not, it will never be a good solution.

In his new position as the Special Advisor for Innovation and Entrepreneurship to the President of Central Washington University, I have seen how J. Eduardo has helped Game On! grow from a pilot program to a solid platform, with the bold goal of reaching one thousand students three years from now. Created in the spring of 2016, Game On! is a public-private partnership supported by the Real Madrid Foundation, Microsoft Corporation, and Central Washington University. It combines computer training with soccer training to foster education through sport as a tool to teach core values. It is the Real Madrid Foundation's first soccer program on the United States' West Coast and the only program of its type in the world affiliated with a university.[2]

---

2   For more information, visit www.cwu.edu/game-on.

From the Real Madrid Foundation, middle and high school students learn the core values of teamwork, self-control, respect, and collaboration. From Microsoft YouthSpark, they learn computational thinking and develop problem-solving skills. This combination of training gives rural Washington students in underserved communities a unique opportunity, teaching them not only college-ready skills, but offering them the hope of being accepted to a university and the hope of a better future.

The work carried out by J. Eduardo at Central Washington University—along with Erica's volunteering—confronts complex issues that are found every day in rural America by Latino students in underserved communities: no hope of graduating from high school, no hope of going to the university. Using the concepts, techniques, and case studies taught in this book, J. Eduardo, Erica, and the University's teams have been crafting sustainable solutions to drive Game On!'s scaling out.

From the first day, J. Eduardo and Erica faced the issues presented head-on, identified optional solutions, and, in the most difficult step of all, convinced all parties that they were protagonists of the program. Today, Game On!, in its second academic year, has six schools and 119 students involved and, by December 2018, about fifteen schools will have a total of 250 students in the program. This is a successful solution, designed for a complex problem, using the checkpoints in the I.D.E.A.S. framework that you will read about in this book.

Today, after almost two years of hard work, lessons were learned, the course was corrected, and the program's success cases have been identified. Students who never thought that they would be able to attend a university are soon to begin their first classes on campus.

In *From Problem Solving to Solution Design: Turning Ideas into Actions,* J. Eduardo Campos and Erica W. Campos—with a combined fifty-year tenure—have made the concepts they developed through their work in several large organizations accessible to all of us. In each I.D.E.A.S. chapter, from Identify to Design, Engage, Act, and Sustain, you will find real cases and ways to resolve the problems inherent in them. The entrepreneurial revolution and its daily changes have not always allowed for the new entrepreneurial environment. The same is true of the business world. This is one reason the book has been written: to help you create sustainable solutions to your problems.

I hope you enjoy this book as much as I did, and that you find the answers that you seek to analyze problems, to craft solutions, and to create a plan to implement them. It is important to remember that a major part of the process is creating a good team that can help implement a sustainable solution, that all members of the team feel they are a necessary part of it, and that without their help the problem could not have been solved.

As I have learned from J. Eduardo and Erica, there is no problem that cannot be solved. TIME TO GAME ON!

Luis Fernando Esteban Bernáldez
Honorary Consul of Spain for Washington and Oregon
Seattle, WA
September 2017

INTRODUCTION

"By three methods we may learn wisdom: First, by reflection,
which is noblest; Second, by imitation, which is easiest;
and Third, by experience, which is the bitterest."

—Confucius

reating solutions to solve problems can often prove very difficult to accomplish, even for seasoned solution designers. Complex organizational problems are identifiable because they have several stakeholders, endless variables, and a myriad of possible solutions. Designing the "right" solution starts by making sure you are addressing the "essential problem"—not just its symptoms. Then, you must walk through several checkpoints in your journey of designing the *best* applicable solution.

This can become a tricky adventure: how do you anticipate potential pitfalls, avoid known mistakes, and increase your chances of success?

As the authors of *From Problem Solving to Solution Design*, we strongly urge you, as the Chinese philosopher Confucius advises, to learn from others who have faced similar challenges. He states that learning from someone else's experience is the wiser and less painful way on this path. We believe that when designing winning solutions for complex problems in your organization you should listen to Confucius, and start your search by understanding how other professionals have dealt with similar issues in the past. Using this book to do so, you will find lessons learned, pragmatic case studies, and references for a deeper dive into any topic of your interest.

In our journey of designing solutions for complex problems in large organizations, we have trailed beaten paths and leveraged others' previous learning. When proven solutions did not match stakeholder expectations, we explored unknown routes. Then, we experimented with innovative approaches, succeeding many times, and failing in so many other cases. But every time we failed, despite feeling frustrated, we stepped back, regrouped with stakeholders, understood the root causes of failure, learned from the lessons presented, took alternative ways, and resumed our pursuit of a solution that would fit the bill until we were able to find the best one applicable. After nailing it down, we felt the exhilaration that often follows success, summing it up with a punch in the air, both fists high, screaming out loud: "We've got it, problem solved!"

Together, we have worked diligently for almost two years to put together this book so that you can learn from professionals who blazed the same path before you. We believe that by sharing the lessons we learned, we will help you become a better Solution Designer for your complex organizational problems.

We wish you success in your quest for the best applicable solutions, and hope that you feel the same joy we describe above when you punch the air at the end of your Solution-Design journey.

WHY SHOULD YOU READ THIS BOOK?

This book was written for *you*, a professional working in either the public or private sector, or in the not-for-profit area. In your role, you might be facing the challenge of designing the best applicable solution for a complex problem.

Our goal is to offer techniques, case studies, and templates to help you find a less painful way to design and implement sustainable solutions to solve some of the more complex problems your organization faces today.

As you will see in the chapters ahead, you will learn how to inform and influence the decision-making process throughout the solution adoption lifecycle—from its ideation to its crafting to convincing others to go along with it. You will also learn that successful solutions are accepted and implemented through the continuous influencing, negotiating, and convincing of people. Because unless your stakeholders are convinced, and your solution matches their expectations, they will go back to prior patterns, face the same issues, and end up with the same lackluster results they reached in the past.

No matter what sector you work in, this approach requires skillful managers, motivated teams, and endless hours of negotiation. Even if you have all that, you might still get nowhere time and again. To increase your chances of success, it is prudent to learn from someone who has been there before you. This can help you avoid pitfalls, take proven paths, and speed up your own problem-solving process.

This book will help you apply what we have learned from our extensive formal training, tireless research, and Solution-Designing experience in addressing everyday situations. We want to provide you with a real-world set of strategies and tactics that will empower you to become a successful Solution Designer who can solve complex organizational problems. You will learn how to identify the problem's root cause and break the issue at hand down into smaller components, therefore developing a series of simpler solutions, which will add up to a broader recommended solution.

This book is not meant to encompass all existing techniques, frameworks, and methodologies. Rather, it is structured as a summarized, pragmatic, and field-proven set of checkpoints to guide you in your journey to design and implement sustainable solutions in your organization. For example, if you need to dive into a given framework—say, implementing internationally accepted internal controls—you might want to explore the COSO framework, which is mentioned in chapter 4.

WHAT IS DIFFERENT ABOUT THIS BOOK?

What differentiates this book from others of a similar nature is the teaching of how to use the organizational *embedded knowledge* to design winning solutions. This is the knowledge found in the existing rules, processes, manuals, organizational culture, codes of conduct, ethics, products, and/or structures. Managing this embedded knowledge is a challenging and complex task, but the organizations that succeed in doing so effectively enjoy a significant competitive advantage.[3] Why? Because this knowledge allows for exploring the significance of relationships between material resources, technologies, roles, formal procedures, and emergent routines.

---

3   Ravindranath Madhavan and Rajiv Grover, "From Embedded Knowledge to Embodied Knowledge: New Product Development as Knowledge Management," *Journal of Marketing* 62, no. 4 (October 1998): 1-12.

We are pleased to share what we have learned over the course of our careers by doing it, by bringing stakeholders along the Solution-Design lifecycle, and by using a pragmatic approach to leverage the existing knowledge in an organization.

As we share throughout the book, to be successful in designing sustainable solutions you cannot lock yourself inside a conference room to craft recommendations, which will be later imposed onto the organization without listening to the people affected by your ideas. You need to avoid pitfalls like reinventing the wheel or coming up with *your own* holy-grail solutions by yourself. Tapping into the existing organizational knowledge, getting the ongoing commitment of others, and communicating results while sharing the credit will help speed up the adoption of your solutions and obtain sustainable results faster than you could ever imagine.

WHAT WAS OUR JOURNEY TO GET TO THIS BOOK?

Several years ago, we were working in different jobs for two large, global organizations. In our roles, we led breakthrough initiatives to address issues caused by what were sometimes first-of-a kind scenarios. It was challenging, a few times frustrating, but in the end rewarding to be stretched beyond our skills and knowledge. We had great mentors, engaged teams, and understanding stakeholders along the way. We both ended up winning public awards for best practices in designing solutions for the complex problems faced by our organizations. At that time, we were focused on information security, governance, risk management, and compliance issues. Due to our public success, we were invited on a regular basis to share Solution-Design experiences in university MBA courses in Brazil, as well as in workshops, conferences, and academic degree programs throughout Latin America and Europe.

Later, as we moved on to other jobs in a different set of global organizations, we received more awards for crafting strategic solutions to address complex problems, this time beyond our initial focus areas. Again, we continued communicating our experiences in recurrent events, professional associations, and academia. Our motivation was to share lessons learned and to learn from others' experiences: we firmly believe there should always be an exchange of insights, including the sharing of failures, with the respective lessons of how to change course and succeed the second time around.

Finally, after moving to the Seattle area and later pursuing our master's degrees in public administration at the Evans School of Public Policy and Governance at the University of Washington, we met Pat Dobel, a professor and mentor, who caught our attention with his lectures on leadership, commitment, and legacy. In his classes, Professor Dobel teaches his students about learning through sharing, giving back, and spreading any knowledge one acquired in life. Why? Because this is part of one's legacy; it's a contribution to other professionals, to other individuals, and to the society. That's when we had an "a-ha" moment: why not package our experiences and the learning we've accumulated over many hours in corporate training, professional association participation, and formal education into a format we could share with others?

And so, we did it. With this book, we tried to capture and share our successes, our failures, and our ensuing course-corrective measures, all in the pursuit of crafting sustainable solutions for complex problems. In doing so, we came up with five critical checkpoints that any Solution Designer must hit to ensure solutions that are successfully envisioned, negotiated with stakeholders, and implemented to last over time.

The best practices gathered in this book consolidate what we have learned in a combined tenure that spans over fifty years of field-tested experience working with corporations, academia, not-for-profit organizations, and governments. Additionally, we have benefitted from thousands of hours of formal training in leading educational organizations. We have worked in multicultural environments across four continents, dealing with intricate public-private-partnerships involving multinational stakeholders spread across different time zones. Managers, clients, and other stakeholders have continuously supported us for years, reassuring us that we were on the right path in the pursuit of highly effective Solution-Design processes. Sure, we may have reached a few dead ends along the way, but we have learned from every opportunity, applying the acquired knowledge to the next solution we designed with our stakeholders.

HOW IS THIS BOOK STRUCTURED?

From Problem Solving to Solution Design: Turning Ideas into Actions is comprised of five chapters, respectively covering each of the check-points recommended to leverage the existing embedded knowledge in your organization, as shown in figure 1-Intro.

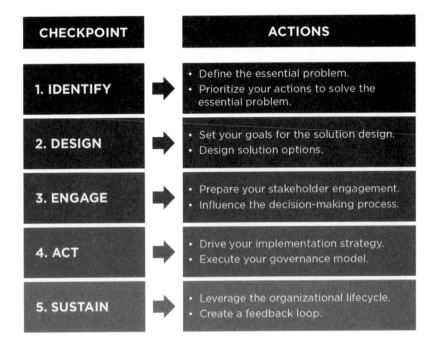

CHECKPOINT		ACTIONS
1. IDENTIFY	➡	• Define the essential problem. • Prioritize your actions to solve the essential problem.
2. DESIGN	➡	• Set your goals for the solution design. • Design solution options.
3. ENGAGE	➡	• Prepare your stakeholder engagement. • Influence the decision-making process.
4. ACT	➡	• Drive your implementation strategy. • Execute your governance model.
5. SUSTAIN	➡	• Leverage the organizational lifecycle. • Create a feedback loop.

Fig. 1-Intro. Chart by J. Eduardo Campos and Erica W. Campos. "I.D.E.A.S. Framework."

Here is a glimpse at what you will find in each chapter:

In **chapter 1: Identify**, you will learn that before you do anything else, you must step back, reflect, and clearly *define the essential problem* you are trying to solve. A couple of case studies illustrate how to do this, including how to use the Five Whys Analysis Method, which helps to isolate the true root-cause of a problem. You can read more about this and other identifying techniques in publications about the Total Quality Management (TQM) movement and its successors, including the *Lean Six Sigma Pocket Toolbook: A Quick Reference Guide to 100 Tools for Improving Quality and Speed.*

We also offer suggestions in this chapter of how to involve your stakeholders, state your goals, and *prioritize your actions to solve the essential problem.* Finally, you will find tips on how complex problems can be broken down into small, manageable components.

In **chapter 2: Design**, you will learn how to *set your goals for Solution Design* and *design solution options.* We also discuss pragmatic risk management strategies.

We share our experiences dealing with complex problems that lead to crises. As you will see, if you take measures to mitigate risks before they lead to a crisis, you can create a sustainable solution and avoid recurrent fire drills (like the fire-brigade exercises, in which the fire alarm sounds, simulating a fire in a building and triggering emergency procedures.)

In **chapter 3: Engage**, we share suggestions on how to *prepare your stakeholder engagement plan and influence the decision-making process.*

This chapter comprises the bulk of the book, because we consider stakeholder engagement to be the core of any successful Solution-Design process. Here, you will learn from real-world scenarios how to identify your key stakeholders, handle objections and match motivations, and assess the decision-making power grid. You will read about the importance of sharing credit with your stakeholders for any successes obtained with your recommendations—the best way to ensure the implemented solutions last longer. You will learn what a marketable solution is, how to prepare your engagement, how to use trade-offs and concessions, and the importance of communicating the decision as clearly and concisely as possible. Finally, you will discover how to get your stakeholders to commit to your solution, how to help your decision-makers decide, and how to use proven practices to get to the decision you want.

Chapter 4: Act shows you how to *drive your implementation strategy*, which will allow for a smooth implementation as well as results measurement. Here you will read real-case scenarios on how to tap into existing control frameworks to coordinate your solution implementation across several types of committees. Finally, this chapter will highlight techniques to help raise awareness about the solution to be adopted.

Chapter 5: Sustain covers a critical milestone in the Solution-Design journey. After all the hard work you have put into identifying the essential problem, designing solution options, engaging stakeholders, and convincing them of the validity of your recommended solution, it is time for you to plan the envisioned sustainability. In fact, during the early stages of option assessment, you might want to consider including criteria that address solution sustainability.

Here, you will learn how to *leverage the organizational lifecycle* to ensure your solution lasts, making the most out of the resources and efforts invested in implementing it. Finally, you will learn how to *create a feedback loop*, guaranteeing that any input received after implementation gets captured and is applied to extend the life of the solution. In many cases, at this stage you might want to start over again, adjusting or improving your solution to keep it relevant to your organization's ever-evolving complex problems.

In this chapter and throughout the rest of the book, you will find pragmatic, real-world case studies which have been anonymized using composite characters, name and/or gender changes, and the change of the respective organizations' sectors, focus, or businesses.

If you want to dig deeper, you can find additional content and references at the end of the book in the appendix.

CALL TO ACTION

Treat this book as your field guide: it offers clear checkpoints for you to assist your organization in designing effective solutions for complex problems. Read it in any order you feel comfortable with, either sequentially or going directly to the information you need help with in your Solution-Design process.

You do not need to make your solutions right the first time. Remember, it is better to try options out, make mistakes, iterate with your stakeholders, correct the course, and rinse and repeat. You shouldn't sit around waiting for the perfect solution to find you—it doesn't happen like that. The only way to arrive at what truly is the "perfect" solution is to try, ask "why," and try again.

In the end, what we want is for you to feel empowered to get out of your seat and dive into Solution-Design options that can help your organization solve problems across organizational borders, time zones, and cultures.

We wish you all the best. Good luck!

J. Eduardo Campos & Erica W. Campos

ONE

IDENTIFY

Define the Essential Problem and Prioritize Your Actions to Solve the Essential Problem

"If I had an hour to solve a problem, I'd spend fifty-five minutes thinking about the problem and five minutes thinking about solutions."

—Albert Einstein

Whenever you are in a situation where you need to solve a problem, resist your instinct to immediately start acting on it. Depending on how big your problem is, the urge to get it out of your way as soon as possible might cloud your perception, preventing you from being effective.

Our recommendation is to kick off the Solution Design for any given complex problem by hitting the initial checkpoint, **identify**, which requires you to take two key actions: (1) define the essential problem, and (2) prioritize your actions to solve the essential problem.

In the first action, defining the essential problem, you should start by stepping back, reflecting, and clearly defining what you are trying to address. This way, you will solve the root cause and not just its symptom, which is the perceived issue (or set of issues) at hand. You might even have more than one problem to solve, which would require more than one solution.

Experience shows that this stepping back enables the problem-solver to have a broader perspective. Ron Heifetz and Marty Linsky used a very interesting analogy in one of their books, *Leadership on the Line: Staying Alive Through the Dangers of Leading*, to explain how to do this. They position the problem-solver as someone dancing in a ballroom, overwhelmed by the band, the music, and the other dancing couples—problem-solvers, they assert, must step off of the dance floor, escape the daily routine, and go up to the balcony. Imagine yourself out on the floor, dancing with everybody else. What you see is just the crowd of people dancing, the band playing, others coming and going and talking.

Now, if you can take a flight of stairs up to the balcony and look at the dance floor from there, you can see it with different eyes. You are looking at the same dancers, you are watching the same band, yet everything looks and sounds different—you can see things and hear tones that you could not when you were on the floor.

Looking down on the party from the balcony gives you the opportunity to see the dance with different lenses. In the same way, if you can detach yourself from a problem and try to see it from a certain distance, you will have a better view of how things interact with each other. Then, you can observe different conflicts going on that you couldn't perceive from the "dance floor" since you were too close to it. You can only observe these things when you are away from the problem's environment, looking at all the stakeholders, the dynamics, the politics, and the individual goals. By broadening your view, you can connect the dots of different issues. Then, even the most complex problems may have simple solutions.

However, you are not able to make decisions and drive actions from the balcony—for that you must return to the dance floor. This back-and-forth movement gives you visibility to the "big picture" without distancing you from where the action occurs. Great managers and leaders have the ability to continually move back and forth between the dance floor and the balcony.

After you have identified the essential problem, you'll need to define which steps come first in the sequence of actions you will take in designing your solution. To prioritize your actions to solve the essential problem you will need to define and apply a set of criteria.

In this chapter, you'll learn how to do this in detail. For both actions, you'll read a case study to illustrate the process.

CHALLENGE 1-1: WHAT IS THE ACTUAL PROBLEM?

When you are tasked with a problem-solving situation, the first step is to identify the real or essential problem. Too often in organizations, people tend to immediately react to the problems in front of them before

> When you are tasked with a problem-solving situation, the first step is to identify the real or essential problem.

they have actually defined the problem's root cause. In many cases, they enter a state of mind we call "fire drill mode," which describes what one does when any problem-solving is approached as a crisis management.

In "fire drill mode," like in the fire brigade exercises, the person facing a complex organizational problem immediately starts putting together task forces to react to the situation instead of questioning what the problem actually is that needs to be solved in the first place. In doing so, the problem symptoms become the focus of any solution being devised. Therefore, the so-called essential problem, which is the root cause of the issue at hand, is not addressed from the start, leading to an escalating loop that keeps people working endlessly on different symptoms for the same problem. Temporary solutions are created and implemented which address some of the symptoms, giving the false impression that the problem is fully solved, only to resurface again down the road.

Moreover, these problem-solvers spend far too much energy and time identifying culpable actors. They get stuck in an endless "investigative assessment," trying to find who the culprits are to blame. This usually leads to finger-pointing among stakeholders (or the "blaming game"), which benefits no one.

> You must move your approach from a problem-solving stance to a Solution-Designing one.

Another issue faced by inexperienced problem-solvers is that they spend too much time finding a *perfect* solution for the problem. Instead, they should get out in the world, talk to their stakeholders, and test any ideas for a solution with them.

If you see yourself in a similar operating mode, then you must move your approach from a problem-solving stance to a Solution-Designing one: try using Solution-Design techniques adapted from Design Thinking (see appendix) and similar methodologies. You must drill down and quickly find the actual problem's root cause, moving your attention to designing optional solutions, testing them with stakeholders to see which work and which do not, iterating, and moving ahead in your Solution-Design process.

Let's start by looking at a case study that is a real-world example of wrongly treating a symptom instead of tackling the essential problem.

CASE STUDY 1-1: BEWARE OF SOLVING THE "SYMPTOMS" INSTEAD OF THE "PROBLEMS"

David Lewis, an experienced problem-solver, was hired by a large international company to revamp its contract management practices.

In his first month on the job, David learned that his department was about to be audited, and that the previous audit did not reflect favorably. The audit had revealed that the company's contracts with ten key suppliers were outdated. The contracts referred to his company's old name, had obsolete requirements that no one was checking anymore, and some of them had even expired. David also learned that, after the audit, the team approved an additional budget to fund a very robust plan to solve the audit finding: a contractor was hired to review all ten contracts and coordinate very complex renegotiations with all parties involved. All ten contracts were updated and then began to be closely monitored by the management team.

In his preparation for the new audit, David decided to check another set of ten key contracts himself: the highest value ones that would probably be included in the auditor's sample for the second audit. These contracts had not been tested during the previous audit. Unsurprisingly, David noticed that these ten contracts had the same issue identified in the previous audit—all of ten of the contracts were outdated. Why? Because the solution adopted after the first audit, updating the ten outdated contracts identified, did not address the essential problem.

David had a few weeks to work with his team to identify the real problem and recommend a definitive solution to leadership. He would need to influence the decision-makers to adopt a definitive solution to the problem.

After the first audit, the team worked on one of the problem's symptoms—the ten outdated contracts—missing the actual problem, the *essential* one, which was the lack of a contract management process. This led the company to have thousands of outdated contracts, not only the ten captured in the first audit sample.

David could decide to keep reacting to audit findings and updating contracts when they were pointed out during audits, or he could choose to influence his management team to fix the actual problem. His task was to convince his company about the importance of implementing a contract management process, which would prove to be more effective in future audits and, more importantly, would protect the company by reducing the risks associated with not having current contracts in place.

CHALLENGE 1-2: IS THERE MORE THAN ONE PROBLEM?

Once you have a good sense of what the essential problem is, be careful to avoid the temptation of immediately making the jump to fix it. As we learned in challenge 1-1, that's how inexperienced problem-solvers behave. Through experience, we have learned that it is better to take a couple more steps to confirm that you have really nailed down the essential problem, the root cause underneath the problem's visible symptoms.

For example, you may have more than one problem in front of you, which would require two different sets of solutions. If there is more than one problem at play, and you have identified only one of them, no matter how good your solution for that one problem is, the other problems will hold you back.

One way to address this is to talk to your stakeholders, share with them your understanding of the complex problem to be solved, ask questions, and iterate. There are a few techniques to use in this case, which are primarily a combination of observation, stakeholder interview, and analysis.

Let's look at an example of how to uncover problems that are intertwined.

CASE STUDY 1-2: YOU DON'T KNOW WHAT YOU DON'T KNOW

Georgia Dupont came to the office and, as she did every morning before going to the kitchen for her fresh cup of coffee, she opened up her company laptop. This time she noticed it was acting erratically, so she decided to call the company's help desk department. After a few minutes of working with the technician, Georgia discovered that a virus had infected her computer. Normally, Georgia was very careful about updating her anti-virus software, but in the past few weeks she had been very busy with a new project and had missed manually updating it. In Georgia's mind, the problem was that her computer had become infected because she had not followed her company's security policies, requiring users to always have an up-to-date anti-virus program on their computers.

Assuming that the problem was completely identified, Georgia agreed with what she thought it was the solution for her problem. After removing the virus, the technician enabled weekly automatic updates in Georgia's computer. Every Monday morning, while Georgia was going to the kitchen for her fresh coffee, the automatic updates would take care of her laptop and avoid any future virus issues. Problem solved!

A few weeks later, Georgia noticed her computer repeating the same erratic behavior. She immediately called the help desk technician and they identified that the computer was once again infected. Georgia and the technician could not understand why the anti-virus software updates had not prevented the computer from becoming infected again. As the technician began interviewing Georgia to better understand what could have happened, he learned that Georgia did not own a personal computer, so she used her laptop in the evenings and on weekends for personal matters, such as home banking. Moreover, digging deeper, the technician learned that Georgia had a teenage son who was a videogame aficionado, and who used his mom's computer to play games online with a few school friends and with some kids from gaming chat rooms.

Georgia and the technician met with Georgia's son and learned that, for a complete gaming experience, some of these websites required Georgia's son to manually disable the anti-virus, which he would forget to turn back on when he was done playing. Georgia was upset because she did not take into account that the apparent "problem," virus infection, had been caused by the fact that she was using her company's laptop for her personal use and had been sharing it with her son. Worse than that, she did not know that her son was accessing non-secure websites and was manually turning off her computer's anti-virus software.

By initially automating the anti-virus updates, Georgia and the technician had treated just one of Georgia's problems. But Georgia actually had three problems at hand: using the computer for personal use, sharing his computer with her son, and not following the company's anti-virus policy.

One solution Georgia adopted was buying a computer for her personal use. Additionally, Georgia educated her son about simple measures he could take, such as how to avoid using non-trusted gaming websites. Then the anti-virus update policy was reinstated in her company's computer, which she now only used for work.

Although this would not likely qualify as a "complex problem," it illustrates the fact that if you just focus on the visible symptom, then you're only going to understand what's happening at a given point in time. It's like comparing a picture and a video. When you look at a problem as a picture in time, you risk solving just the symptoms. But when you look at the problem as a video, you are considering what *happened*, what *is happening*, and what *could happen* in the future; it's a more comprehensive approach that helps you to better define the essential problem and, thus, come up with the appropriate solution.

CHALLENGE 1-3: WHY IS IT A PROBLEM?

Due to the fast-paced nature of the modern life, some people tend to rush to quickly solve problems, which might end up creating recurring problems, or more problems that beget other problems. Too often, they jump in on how to solve a problem and forget to ask first what the problem is and, second, why the problem exists in the first place.

> The question becomes not only *"How* do we define the problem?" but also, *"Why* is the problem happening?" Surprisingly that's the question most people *do not* ask.

The question becomes not only *"How* do we define the problem?" but also, *"Why* is the problem happening?" Surprisingly that's the question most people *do not* ask.

There's a technique called the Five Whys, developed in 1930s by Sakichi Toyoda (founder of Toyota Industries Co., Ltd, which would later become the Toyota Motor Corporation). The theory basically says you should not stop at the first answer that you get when you ask "why," because there are probably more layers under that. You can identify parts of the problem or problems, then get to the root cause if you *keep asking* "why." If there is another tier of "why" that you can answer, then you have not yet identified your final problem. You should keep asking "why" until you get to the root cause.

Let's go back to David and his contract management problem in Case Study 1–1:

1. Why didn't the vendors have updated contracts?

   a. Because changes in the business environment (e.g., the company's name changed) made the contracts obsolete.

2. Why?

   b. Because no one was tasked to regularly update the contracts.

3. Why?

   c. Because there wasn't a process in place to establish the need to update contracts.

4. Why?

   d. Because there was no requirement to do so.

5. Why?

   e. Because there was a policy gap.

By asking the Five Whys, David got to the essential problem: his company lacked a contract management policy to solve the contract obsolescence issue. Therefore, he created a policy with the requirements for a process to ensure that contracts are updated. Only then he was able to solve the *essential* problem.

In our next case study, we'll see a real-world example about how to create a structured Five Whys table and its respective action plan.

CASE STUDY 1-3: WHY, WHY, WHY, WHY, WHY ...

Recently hired to revamp the corporate security department of a major wholesale company that focused on selling jewelry to fashion store chains, Alicia Williams decided it was time to rock the boat.

In her first month, she prepared a list with the action items she thought were the most pressing, including the ones shared by the company's leadership and her peers during her hiring process. On her list, she included what partners and clients had told her and her team during the several walkthroughs she carried out at the company's main facilities.

One of the top issues was a complaint that came up during her visit to the company's biggest operations center. There, vendors, clients, and other visitors were routinely hosted as business meetings were held at that facility. The issue: the waiting time at the center's main reception desk ranged from forty to seventy minutes, just to get a badge and be escorted to the meeting destination.

The tipping point came when the chief procurement officer of a leading chain store, one of the company's top three clients, had to wait almost an hour to be granted entry. He was furious, felt snubbed, and almost cancelled the contract, which would have been a significant hit to the company's bottom line. News of the incident made it to the boardroom, and Alicia was told to make solving this "security problem" a priority.

Because the logistics center also hosted sensitive operations— such as strategic planning, the visitor screening and access control were done thoroughly at the center's reception desk. The visitor screening consisted of a background check using a public database, where the visitor was checked for any previously reported security incidents. Then, access control would provide entry to the facilities on a need-to-know basis (e.g., access to strategic planning was limited to a by-invitation list only).

Reflecting on the issue at hand, Alicia did not feel certain about the root cause for the waiting time. Stating, "It is a security issue," seemed too vague. She decided to use the Five Whys technique and asked the first "why": "Why is this long waiting time happening in the main reception area?"

FIVE WHYS TECHNIQUE: CASE STUDY APPLICATION

Let's have a look at the steps taken:

Why 1: Why the huge wait time?

From her interviews with management and visitors, Alicia confirmed that the visitor's access processing is too slow. Let's start building a table with Alicia's findings for "whys" and the answers.

WHYS	ANSWERS
Why 1: Why is this huge waiting time happening in the main reception area?	The visitor access processing is too slow.

Fig. 1-1. Why 1 versus answer.

Then, Alicia asked the next "why":

Why 2: Why is the visitor access processing too slow?

Alicia realized she needed more information to get the right answers, and decided to spend some time at the reception desk to observe the visitor influx for herself.[4]

The next Monday morning, Alicia arrived early at the company center's main reception area. She asked to speak with the reception-

---

4   Observation is a great way to gather fresh and unbiased information. Nothing replaces looking in the eyes of your audience, feeling the heat of the environment, and taking in the facts as they happen before your eyes.

ist, as a stakeholder, who had been working longer with the current process.[5] After managing the anxiety caused by having Alicia, the security director, directly asking her questions, Selma Harris—the most experienced receptionist—opened her heart and confirmed Alicia's suspicions: for the visitor screening, the receptionists used a very old application, which had been discontinued by the original IT vendor long ago. It accessed an old online database, with a very slow connection time. Many times, the system just hung up or the screen froze, with no explanation, causing the data entered to be lost, and requiring that it all be keyed in again.

Also, because the visitor screening application software was outdated, it did not work in tandem with the modern access control system, requiring the data entry of the visitor's personal information to be repeated after the initial background check was done. Because of "savings" during the procurement process, the access control system could not store the visitor list for more than three days, requiring the recurring data entry for regular visitors, who became annoyed at having to repeat their data every visit.

Alicia, then, updated her table:

WHYS	ANSWERS
Why 1: Why is this huge waiting time happening in the main reception area?	The visitor access processing is too slow.
Why 2: Why is the visitor access processing too slow?	Some of the components (e.g., visitor screening) or the entire visitor access processing practice is broken.

Fig. 1-2. Why 2 versus answer.

---

5   Stakeholder interviewing is another great way to get unbiased information because you learn directly from the source.

With this information in hand, and after confirming that there were three receptionists at the front desk (enough to deal with the observed volume), Alicia asked the third "why":

Why 3: Why was the reception staff not compensating for the broken visitor access processing?

Selma, the receptionist, replied that the staff had to cover for another two reception areas—therefore, staffing could go from three receptionists to one at any time, causing major delays in visitor registration. Moreover, the receptionists did not communicate well with each other, contributing to the imbalance of staff.

WHYS	ANSWERS
Why 1: Why is this huge waiting time happening in the main reception area?	The visitor access processing is too slow.
Why 2: Why is the visitor access processing too slow?	Some of the components (e.g., visitor screening) or the entire visitor access processing process is broken.
Why 3: Why is the reception staff not compensating for the broken visitor access processing?	The staff has to cover for another two receptions—therefore, the receptionist count could go from three to one at any time, causing major delays in visitor registration.

Fig. 1-3. "Why" 3 versus answer.

Alicia's next question followed suit:

Why 4: Why did the staff have to cover for another two receptions?

Because the other reception areas would become even more backlogged by midday, with people lined up outside waiting to be granted access.

WHYS	ANSWERS
Why 1: Why is this huge waiting time happening in the main reception area?	The visitor access processing is too slow.
Why 2: Why is the visitor access processing too slow?	Some of the components (e.g., visitor screening) or the entire visitor access processing process is broken.
Why 3: Why is the reception staff not compensating for the broken visitor access processing?	The staff has to cover for another two receptions—therefore, the receptionist count could go from three to one at any time, causing major delays in visitor registration.
Why 4: Why does the staff have to cover for another two receptions?	The other receptions would become backlogged by midday, with people lining up outside waiting to be granted access.

Fig. 1-4. Why 4 versus answer.

Finally, Alicia closed the Five Whys with the following question:

Why 5: Why would the other receptions become backlogged by midday?

According to Selma, the other reception areas used a simpler software version for the front desk operations, one even slower than the software used in the main reception area computers. By midday, these bare-bones applications would begin crashing, leading to longer waiting lines. To make it worse, the staff lacked communications skills, not being able to coordinate among themselves about who should work where.

WHYS	ANSWERS
Why 1: Why is this huge waiting time happening in the main reception area?	The visitor access processing is too slow.
Why 2: Why is the visitor access processing too slow?	Some of the components (e.g., visitor screening) or the entire visitor access processing process is broken.
Why 3: Why is the reception staff not compensating for the broken visitor access processing?	The staff has to cover for another two receptions—therefore, the receptionist count could go from three to one at any time, causing major delays in visitor registration.
Why 4: Why does the staff have to cover for another two receptions?	The other receptions would become backlogged by midday, with people lining up outside waiting to be granted access.
Why 5: Why would the other receptions crash by midday?	The receptions would crash due to bare-bone applications as well as lack of staff training to improve communications among receptionists.

Fig. 1-5. Why 5 versus answer.

With the Five Whys answered, Alicia finished her observation and interviewing exercise with a good understanding of the initial, broader issue (excessive waiting time at the center's main reception). She also had a good grasp of the respective answers to address it, because she was able to break the broader issue into smaller pieces.

Figure 1-6 shows Alicia's conclusions and recommendations to solve the initially reported problem.

ISSUES	ANSWERS	MITIGATING ACTIONS
Why 1: Why is this huge waiting time happening in the main reception?	The visitor access processing is too slow.	• Improve the access control processing time. • Define success metrics, to be revised every six months. • Revise and update the visitor access procedure.
Why 2: Why is the visitor access processing too slow?	Some of the components (e.g., visitor screening) or the entire visitor access processing process is broken.	• Update or replace the visitor screening software. • Upgrade the access control application so that it can store at least four weeks of data for the regular visitors. • Retrain staff to operate the new software.
Why 3: Why is the reception staff not compensating for the broken visitor access processing?	The staff had to cover for another two receptions—therefore, the receptionist count could go from three to one at any time, causing major delays in visitor registration.	• Revise contingency procedures for dynamic reception reinforcement.
Why 4: Why does the staff have to cover for another two receptions?	The other receptions would become backlogged by midday, with people lining up outside waiting to be granted access.	• Same as previous action. • Set a three-people shift for each reception.
Why 5: Why would the other receptions crash by midday?	The receptions would crash due to bare-bone applications as well as lack of staff training to improve communications among receptionists.	• Invest in software updates as in previous action items, adopting a standard version for all receptions. • Train reception staff to improve communication skills.

Fig. 1-6. Reported issues, answers, and mitigating actions.

In summary, Alicia took the initial issue, used the Five Whys technique to break it down into smaller problems, and then came up with actions to mitigate the component of the broader issue.

She used additional techniques to gather information, such as Walkthrough, Observation, and Interviewing, to ensure that she would get unbiased information.

Because the world is not perfect, there is no endless budget for Alicia to mitigate all issues at once. Therefore, she needs to prioritize the action items, define an implementation plan, measure results, and ask for more resources. You will learn how to do that later in this book.

CHALLENGE 1-4: TOO BIG TO WORK IT OUT

Complex problems must be broken down into small, easier-to-understand components. Addressing the "big problem" in smaller pieces helps you to step back more often, measure small successes by addressing the smaller pieces, and course-correct if necessary. For that to be successful, you still need to prioritize which of the smaller pieces you want to address first, meaning you need to prioritize which of the smaller problems and respective proposed solutions you want to tackle first.

The question becomes, "How do you prioritize?" For example, by distinguishing between *important* and *urgent* problems, you can create a simple chart. This way, you will have four quadrants:

- Low Importance/Low Urgency
- High Importance/Low Urgency
- Low Importance/High Urgency
- High Importance/High Urgency

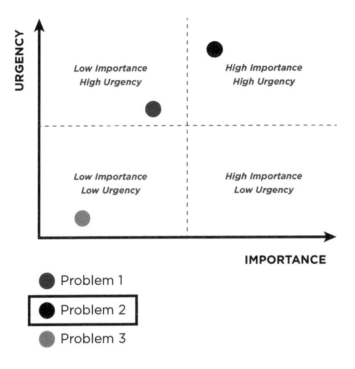

Fig. 1-7. Multiple concurrent problems to be solved—one prioritization strategy.

Then you can fill the quadrants with the information in hand, mapping it out to visualize the problems you should prioritize.

Importance can be measured in terms of cost, in terms of effectiveness, in terms of political support, or in terms of administrative visibility. For *urgency*, you can use implementation time, or risk exposure (e.g., if the problem is a matter of reputational or legal risk).

After establishing the prioritization criteria, you might want to attribute weights to the items you defined. What piece of criteria should weigh more in your problem-prioritization process? Would it be immediacy? Maybe current cost levels?

The more critical the item is for you, the higher the weight. Keep it simple, and it should work even for the most complex situations.

Let's have a look at a case study to understand how this works in the real world.

CASE STUDY 1-4: SLICE, DICE, AND PRIORITIZE

In the wake of the 2008 US real estate crisis, Kate Hernandez was hired as a consultant to assist the CEO of a large house building company with his structuring of a business turnaround strategic plan. Then, the CEO would submit it and get it approved by the company's board.

The problem presented to Kate had been articulated around excessive costs for the new reality of a shrinking housing market. Therefore, she kicked off her consulting engagement by checking the company's public financial data so that she could get herself familiarized with the numbers supporting the plan to be structured.

However, after a few days of reading several financial reports, Kate was still struggling to find costs to be cut. She started wondering if the company might be already lean enough. Stepping back, Kate reflected on the problem handed over to her. What if it were much more complex than initially presented? What if she, in fact, had more than one problem to deal with?

Kate sought advice from Lena Farber—a twenty-year company veteran and the Chief Financial Officer (CFO)—who offered additional context of the company's situation. Kate learned that the CEO had just another year left in his current contract, and that he was being pressured to show quick results, which would lead the board of directors to either renew his contract for another term or get another CEO to do his job.

In this dragging economic scenario, senior executives in house building companies—struggling to show result improvements—had been promoting drastic cost-cutting as the panacea for business recovery. Many competitors, hindered by cost-cutting to the bone, ended up going out of business. In Lena's assessment, the current CEO was about to repeat the formula as a risky bet to secure his job contract renewal. Additionally, Kate was told that the company's founder and former CEO had been replaced by the current executive after speaking against this cost-reduction push. Moreover, Lena shared that the former CEO had publicly clashed with the board, pushing for an alternative three-year investment plan, based on his conclusion that the company should not be downsized. Quite the opposite, it should invest in a few areas while cutting costs in a much smaller scale, just to live through the crisis and to better prepare for fresh opportunities which should follow a market recovery down the road.

The board said it didn't have time for a three-year plan, replaced the CEO with the current one, and doubled-down on the cost-cutting option. Kate got her hands on a copy of the three-year investment plan, which had been originally compiled by Lena, and decided to interview several other executives also involved in the plan preparation. With that, Kate learned more about how the different divisions within the company would be affected by both directions the company could go: (1) either radically downsize and risk dying, or (2) cost-cut less and live to fight another day—maybe even grow.

Wrapping up the field interviews, Kate compared her findings with Lena's document and realized that the organization's financial difficulties could be better dealt with by peeling away the onion, which meant breaking the complex problem at hand into a few smaller problems which could then be easily addressed—and that was what she did.

- Initial problem: the company finances are bleeding, with drastically reduced revenue, high costs, and no end in sight for the current housing crisis.

- Problem components:

  → Business units have overlapping sales roles.

  → Business unit costs are higher than their respective revenue.

  → Some business units have no revenue at all.

  → No rental properties are part of the business.

Next, Kate listed the prioritization criteria she would use to come up with which problem should be solved first. Then, she put values and weights to each piece of criteria and built a table with them and the four main culprits for the company's dire financial situation, shown in figure 1-8.

PROBLEM SOLVING PRIORITIZATION

Complex Problem: components vs. weights	Importance (low = 1; high = 3)	Urgency (low = 1; high = 3)	Future recovery (weight: 3) (low = 1; medium = 3; high = 5)	Quick win (weight: 2) (low = 1; medium = 3; high = 5)
A. Business units have overlapping sales roles	1	1	3	1
B. Business units costs are way higher than revenue	3	3	5	3
C. Business units have no current revenue	3	3	1	5
D. Portfolio: no rental properties considered	1	3	5	1

Fig. 1-8. Problem-Solving Prioritization.

Then, Kate did some calculation by multiplying weights and adding up the cells:

➡ A. Business units have overlapping sales roles. [1+1+(3x3) +(1x2)] = **13**

➡ B. Business unit costs are higher than their respective revenue. [3+3+(5x3) +(3x2)] = **27**

➡ C. Some business units have no revenue at all. [3+3+(1x3) +(5x2)] = **19**

➡ D. No rental properties are part of the business. [1+3+(5x3) +(1x2)] = **21**

Finally, Kate got to the following order for her problem-solving prioritization:

- → B. Business unit costs are higher than their respective revenue: **27**

- → D. No rental properties are part of the business: **21**

- → C. Some business units have no revenue at all: **19**

- → A. Business units have overlapping sales roles: **13**

After four months of hard work, with the right information in hand, a case made for each problem component, and with the support of key company executives, Kate was able to convince the CEO to combine a lighter cost-cutting approach to investing in expanding the company's business with adding rental properties in the sales portfolio.

The plan was approved after a thorough negotiation with the board. Business units that were operating in the red were quickly reorganized or closed. Others that had no revenue faced a similar fate. Later, roles and responsibilities were revamped, and the new portfolio was built by a merger with a smaller rental property company, bringing new blood into the ranks and some new revenue streams.

After just five years, the resulting company became the absolute leader in rental properties, which helped it come through the rough economic times. Now, several years later, with house building coming back to its glorious old days, the company is much more prepared to run its business.

Reflecting on this positive scenario, Kate concluded that cost-cutting alone would not have brought the company to its position today. She was successful in her quest to change the CEO's mind because she was able to identify at the beginning that the problem she was hired to solve was actually made up of several problems. Also, she learned from different people and their perspectives by getting information from different teams, absorbing the dynamics between them by working with them (at the dance floor) while detaching herself when she needed to broaden her own perspective (going to the balcony).

Finally, by identifying all the problems the company really had and breaking them down into smaller pieces, she was able to address them and prioritize solving them over time. While her solution may not have been what the CEO was looking for at the beginning, it was the one that helped the company to thrive in a negative economic scenario.

KEY TIPS FOR CHAPTER ONE:

1. Define the problem. And remember, you might have more than one.

2. Ask the Five Whys. This will help you to identify the root cause of the essential problem—what you really need to focus on and solve.

3. Involve the stakeholders. Listen to all the players, ask the right questions, dance on the floor with them, and then go to the balcony to get a different perspective of the same crowd.

4. Break down the problem into smaller ones and prioritize your actions to solve the essential problem.

TWO

DESIGN

Set Your Goals for the Solution Design and Design Solution Options

"I haven't failed. I've just found ten thousand ways that won't work."

—Thomas Edison

Setting goals and assessing options are critical components for any effective Solution-Design process. This, when well thought out, increases the odds for having the essential problem addressed by sustainable solutions.

It's not unusual to find yourself in a situation where the problems you identified are part of a dynamic environment, affected by constant changes that require you to revisit your goals and your options regularly. This is where technology and software can be very helpful in making sure everything is being tracked and recorded appropriately without any information getting lost.

While these changes are occurring, it's important to have a process that allows you to be consistent with your approach, even in the most unstable scenarios, to help you to focus on the essential problem you need to address—the one you identified as the root cause of your headaches. In addition to technology, using risk management concepts can be a very effective way to help you keep consistency throughout the design process. You will be able to define criteria to prioritize the problems to solve, evaluate solution options, and avoid the trap of ending up in an eternal crisis management— what we call "fire drill" mode.

Let's unfold these concepts.

CHALLENGE 2-1: DEFINING THE SOLUTION GOALS

After you have clarified which problem has a higher priority to be addressed it is time to work on it with your stakeholders. First, you will need to confirm that everyone is on the same page. You can use any framework or methodology you want to determine your stakeholders' needs, such as Design Thinking. This is a method for the practical, creative resolution of problems and creation of solutions that was adapted for business purposes by Stanford University's David M. Kelley. Kelley later founded the design consultancy IDEO, which guides Solution Designers to work with stakeholders to understand their needs/problems, then develop potential solutions that would address these issues.

When it is time to make a decision about which alternative you should pick, we highly recommended that you use one of the several methodologies for decision-making to assess alternatives to address these concerns. One of the most well-known is the PrOACT, which allows you to put numbers to options, thus enabling you to assess them and choose the best one to solve the problem at hand.[6]

To illustrate, let's follow Faith Diaz, who is in charge of defining the decision-making for a major problem by using a methodology she selected for that problem. For the sake of the case study, we will not cover Design Thinking or the creation of prototypes, focusing instead on the decision-making process in front of Faith.

CASE STUDY 2-1: CREATE OBJECTIVES OUT OF STAKEHOLDER CONCERNS TO CREATE EFFECTIVE SOLUTIONS

Cloud4All, Inc. went through a major business reorganization in early 2011, changing its management solutions to use cloud technologies, which enabled it to cut costs, accelerate growth, and respond to customer needs influenced by emerging tech trends, such as big data, mobile technology, and social media. This could bring tremendous potential economic impact as new cloud-based businesses, jobs, and services emerge. Moreover, the ensuing investments to enable the company's transformation into a cloud-based solution provider could benefit not only Cloud4All, but also the countries where it had presence. Interestingly, by 2011, emerging markets had recovered faster from the 2008 crisis. However, since they were used to investing only in developed markets, Cloud4All faced the same issue as other corporations based in mature markets, such as the United States: it faced lack of alignment with the national aspirations of these emerging market countries.

---

6   John Hammond, Ralph Keeney, and Howard Raiffa, *Smart Choices: A Practical Guide to Making Better Life Decisions*, Crown Business, 2002.

Cloud4All was perceived as just another foreign player—an outsider. With a newly revised charter and strategy, the company decided to change this perception and show it had its skin-in-the-game: they would invest in a public fund to foster innovation in emerging markets. This fund would be part of a broader program, a public-private partnership with local stakeholders—including governments—which should help Cloud4All in aligning with the national aspirations in emerging markets. This partnership would create a collaborative cluster, with the goal of investing in cloud-based technology startups. This would foster local innovation, create jobs, and grow the economy—music to the ears of these countries' leaderships. Besides providing seed funding to the entrepreneurs, in this business acceleration model, expert mentors would guide the infant companies to grow and enter the mainstream market. Candidate companies must have a maximum annual revenue of $3 million USD, must have spent three years or more in the market, and must have at least one formal customer. When Faith Diaz, a former serial entrepreneur, now working for Cloud4All, heard about it, she pushed her leadership hard and got the job to lead the company's participation in the new program, which they agreed to with a caveat: she was given just twelve months to push at least ten companies through the business acceleration funnel, from the fund build-up to the participant companies' selection to their mentorship to their first public presentation (called Start-up Demo Day).

Empowered by her management, Faith rolled up her sleeves and went to work. She had read about newly created concepts written in an article titled "Creating Shared Value" by Michael Porter and Mark Kramer for *Harvard Business Review* in 2011 and decided to apply them, confirming the three goals for the new collaboration: (1) foster innovation through investment in technology start-ups, (2) create jobs, and (3) grow the local economy. With clearly communicated goals and the economy slowly coming back, Faith was able to bring to the table investors, local governments, public agencies, and non-profits focused on small businesses and job creation, although most of the participants were still skeptical about the multi-stakeholder model she was enthusiastically putting together.

CRITICAL DECISION-MAKING: FIRST THINGS FIRST

One of the first major decisions the stakeholders had to make as a group was picking the location to incorporate the public fund created to sustain the Emerging Markets Program, led by Faith. Their decision rested on the question: "Where to create an Emerging Markets' Innovation Fund?"

As one would expect, the first impulse the stakeholders had was to immediately start debating the candidate locations for the fund. However, Faith, an experienced Solution Designer, called out the need for capturing "everyone's input," which is technically known as "expectations and concerns," before doing anything.

Because she had read the excellent book *Smart Choices: A Practical Guide to Making Better Life Decisions* by John Hammond, Ralph Keeney, and Howard Raiffa, Faith decided to interview each of her stakeholders, then gathered them in a room to double-check each one's viewpoints to drive consensus. Below are the questions Faith prepared her stakeholders to answer together:

- What do I really want?

- What are my hopes for this fund?

- What are my goals?

- What do I need see addressed?

This was a clever approach.

Below, you can find the list of concerns consolidated by Faith Diaz and the stakeholders she spoke with, which covers what issues the location should address for the fund creation to be successful:

- lack of facilities to host start-ups

- costs spiraling out of control

- income shortage causing inability to deliver on commitments

- lack of start-up mentors

- non-existant local government support

- disconnected from country's agenda and interests

- not focused on local subsidiary goals or company's priorities

- lack of focus leading to boiling the ocean

- mistakenly selecting tech start-ups not up to the challenge

- unhealthy local innovation environment (high piracy rates, no guarantees for intellectual property rights, no candidate start-ups in the pipeline, weak academic ecosystem)

- no venture capital players aboard

- no reputable partners available or interested

Before even getting to the actual location selection process, this list was used to feed an ensuing workshop with the whole group where stakeholders could voice their values, specific needs, and aspirations for the fund.

Let's have a look at the results of this workshop, noting that italicized words are wording used by the stakeholders.

Stakeholder Workshop Results— Values and Objectives

From Cloud4All, Inc.'s perspective, investments in technology startups should prioritize the newly defined company focus on cloud-based management solutions. Also, it should happen in the top emerging markets where it has presence, leveraging its local subsidiary staff. For all stakeholders, picking *markets with a ripe innovation ecosystem* would help maximize chances of success—it is key to have abundant candidate startups at the beginning of the funnel. This must be considered hand-in-hand with a steady flow of new professionals coming from science, technology, engineering, and mathematics (STEM) courses, prepared in an academic environment with highly reputable universities. Public policies in those markets should be in place to foster innovation (e.g., tax-breaks for startups and public funding for smaller technology players). *Intellectual property laws* must exist to protect inventors/entrepreneurs, and a *trustworthy national financial system* should be in place to back investments in innovation. Considering it is a public-private partnership, the fund should reflect *stakeholder priority alignment*. By matching the country's agenda, it would ensure that it draws local government support. Moreover, it should be connected to the company's local subsidiary priorities. Finally, it is critical that the fund is *self-sustainable*. It should keep *operational costs* low and locally funded, and rely on *available internal resources* as well as on *external investment sources*. *Venture capital's seed money* and *strong reputable local partners* should be previously identified and committed to the fund operations.

The prior list was used together with the workshop results above to generate the following table using the same methodology earlier described (PrOACT).

OBJECTIVES	SUB-OBJECTIVES
A. STAKEHOLDER PRIORITY ALIGNMENT	Country's national aspirations matching
	Local government supported
	Connection with stakeholder subsidiaries' priorities
B. RIPE ECOSYSTEM IN CANDIDATE MARKET	Abundance of candidate technology start-ups
	Academic environment with highly reputable universities
	Steady flow of new professionals coming from STEM courses
	Innovation fostering public policies in place
	Mature intellectual property environment
	Identified partner in the financial system
C. SELF-SUSTAINABLE	Existing foreign investment sources
	Available venture capital's seed money
	Available resources from local stakeholder
	Operational costs funding
	Committed funding from local partners

Fig. 2-1. Objectives and sub-objectives for where to create an emerging markets' innovation fund.

CHALLENGE 2-2: ASSESS YOUR SOLUTION OPTIONS AND PICK THE BEST ONE

After you were able to craft the objectives and sub-objectives for your solution based on your stakeholders' concerns and values, you will need to gauge these against potential alternatives to find the best option to address the problem in front of you.

During the initial interviews with your stakeholders, individually and in a group, you have likely elicited a few alternative solutions. The methodology applied in the following case study, 2-2, is helpful in this phase, as well. Here you will learn how to elicit these other options and, moreover, you will learn how to compare alternative solutions, including how to carry out trade-offs among them.

Let's continue following Faith Diaz in her quest to help her stakeholders pick a location to create an emerging markets fund for startups.

CASE STUDY 2-2: NUMBERS DON'T LIE

After Faith interviewed her stakeholders, led a couple of workshops, and was able to create a table with objectives and sub-objectives based on her stakeholders' concerns and values, it was time to move to the next step. Faith went back to the drawing board to play with the alternative sites for the fund, which had been also captured during the stakeholders' workshop. The result is a list of options for each site's potential location and the respective justifications—leaving open which country, region, or continent should be selected because of several available options in each region:[7]

1. **New Zealand**: With a vibrant technology startup environment, the country reminds us of technological breakthroughs since the blockbuster *Avatar*'s filming.

2. **Africa**: Sub-Saharan Africa bears one of the highest mobile phone adoption rates worldwide, and a fast-growing broadband usage rate. For now, the stakeholders decided to leave open which country should be selected because there were several available options in the region.

3. **Argentina**: Argentina has one of the highest mobile phone adoption scores worldwide as well as a fast-growing broadband usage rate. Buenos Aires has a vibrant technology startup environment, fostered by public policies and venture capital presence.

---

7   Country names and regions are used for illustration purposes only.

Let's see how the previous table, figure 2-1, evolved with the addition of these options.

OBJECTIVES	SUB-OBJECTIVES	OPTIONS		
		1. Invest in public fund in **New Zealand**	2. Invest in public fund in **Africa**	3. Co-invest in public fund in **Argentina**
A. STAKE-HOLDER PRIORITY ALIGNMENT (YES=3; NO=0)	Country's national aspirations matching			
	Local government supported			
	Connection with sub-sidiaries' priorities			
B. RIPE ECOSYSTEM IN CANDIDATE MARKETS (HIGH=3; MEDIUM=2; LOW=1)	Abundance of candidate technology start-ups			
	Academic environment with highly reputable universities			
	Steady flow of new professionals coming from STEM courses			
	Innovation fostering public policies in place			
	Mature intellectual property environment			
	Identified partner in the financial system			
C. SELF-SUSTAINABLE	Existing foreign invest-ment sources			
	Available venture capital's seed money			
	Available resources from local stakeholder			
	Operational costs funding			
	Committed funding from local partners			
TOTAL =		Score total and USD amount	Score total and USD amount	Score total and USD amount

Fig. 2-2. Options table for the creation of an emerging markets' innovation fund.

The next step for Faith was to add a range of values as well as the weight given by the stakeholders to each line (sub-objectives) for each of the options:

Values and Weighting

a. stakeholder priority alignment (a critical objective, thus gets a bigger weight for "Yes"): "Yes" = 3; "No" = 0

b. ripe ecosystem in candidate market: high = 3; medium = 2; low = 1

c. self-sustainable: resource in USD currency that is/will be available at the fund creation announcement

With that, Faith could assign a numeric value to each option by adding up the respective scores. She has also added the known dollar amounts for the lines of objective C, "self-sustainable," to allow for "trade-off negotiation" later.

The new table looks like this:

OBJECTIVES	SUB-OBJECTIVES	OPTIONS		
		New Zealand	Africa	Argentina
A. STAKE-HOLDER PRIORITY ALIGNMENT (YES=3; NO=0)	Country's national aspirations matching	0	3	3
	Local government supported	0	3	3
	Connection with subsidiaries' priorities	0	3	3
B. RIPE ECOSYSTEM IN CANDIDATE MARKETS (HIGH=3; MEDIUM=2; LOW=1)	Abundance of candidate technology start-ups	2	2	2
	Academic environment with highly reputable universities	2	1	1
	Steady flow of new professionals coming from STEM courses	2	2	2
	Innovation fostering public policies in place	3	2	2
	Mature intellectual property environment	3	1	1
	Identified partner in the financial system	3	2	3
C. SELF-SUSTAINABLE	Existing foreign investment sources	$350K	$4M	$5M
	Available venture capital's seed money	$500K	$3M	$2M
	Available resources from local stakeholder	$100K	$150K	$1M
	Operational costs funding	$500K	$400K	$500K
	Committed funding from local partners	$1M	$1M	$500K
TOTAL =		15 and $2,45M	19 and $8,55M	20 and $9M

Fig. 2-3. Options table with values and weighting for the creation of an emerging markets' innovation fund.

As you may be realizing, Faith came a long way from the initial concerns voiced by her stakeholders, representing both real and potential problems. Anchored on the principles of the decision-making framework PrOACT, Faith was able to put numbers to subjective concepts and opinions.

This is great; now Faith is ready to move ahead with her decision-making process and zero in on the best solution for the stated problem—a truly complex one because of the sheer number of stakeholders, options, and criteria.

CHALLENGE 2-3: MAKE THE RIGHT CHOICES WHEN IT IS TIME

When you are designing solutions for your organization, you may come to a point in your decision-making process where the options you have in your hands are strong ones, therefore making it tricky to make a choice.

That is when you need to count on a verifiable approach to bet on the best solution for your organization's complex problem. Remember, you will likely have to explain why you did not pick this or that solution, because some of your stakeholders might get somewhat attached to their initial choices.

You can find several methodologies and frameworks to help you in this phase, but we strongly recommend adapting PrOACT, discussed previously, to match your needs. The authors teach how to compare the final options, negotiate trade-offs, and renegotiate stakeholder commitment to solving the problem.

Let's wrap up Faith's decision-making process in the following case study so that you can learn from a real-world case.

CASE STUDY 2-3: THE CRITICAL TURN IN THE CRANK

Now Faith could see that by comparing the total numeric score as well as the total amount of available funding for the three alternative site locations she could move ahead with her decision-making process. It became clear that Africa and Argentina were both good options, and that New Zealand should be eliminated both because of its lower numeric score and because of its lower amount of available funding at the planned announcement. Her updated table is below.

OBJECTIVES	SUB-OBJECTIVES	OPTIONS	
		Africa	Argentina
A. STAKEHOLDER PRIORITY ALIGNMENT (YES = 3; NO = 0)	Country's national aspirations matching	3	3
	Local Government supported	3	3
	Connection with subsidiaries' priorities	3	3
B. RIPE ECOSYSTEM IN CANDIDATE MARKETS (HIGH = 3; MEDIUM = 2; LOW = 1)	Abundance of candidate technology start-ups	2	2
	Academic environment with highly reputable universities	1	1
	Steady flow of new professionals coming from STEM courses	2	2
	Innovation fostering public policies in place	2	2
	Mature intellectual property environment	1	1
	Identified partner in the financial system	2	3
C. SELF-SUSTAINABLE	Existing foreign investment sources	$4M	$5M
	Available venture capital's seed money	$3M	$2M
	Available resources from local stakeholder	$150K	$1M
	Operational costs funding	$400K	$500K
	Committed funding from local partners	$1M	$550K
TOTAL =		19 & $8.55M	20 & $9M

Fig. 2-4. Options table with site location finalists for the creation of an emerging markets' innovation fund.

Faith took the previous table, without New Zealand, and went back to her stakeholders for their help in deciding between Africa and Argentina. This is the point of "trade-off negotiation," where the interested parties offer to negotiate (trade-off) improvements in their options to even out or outweigh the others. In some cases, this allows for a trade-off ("swap") between columns, eliminating options by making scores/values the same for two or more of them. How did trade-off negotiation work for Faith's project? As you can see in the previous table (figure 2-4), Africa and Argentina scored very closely (nineteen and twenty, respectively), and have available resources that differ by only $450,000 (in favor of Argentina). Going back to her stakeholders, Faith received improved offers from each party supporting either Africa or Argentina, as indicated below:

- Supporters of the Africa location offered to equal the number of financial partners of Argentina (making their score go from two to three. See the solid-line box in figure 2-5.), thereby evening the score (both Africa and Argentina would get twenty).

- Supporters of the Argentina location offered to significantly raise the dollar amount of resources and shared that the local government was soon going to announce a public-private partnership to improve innovation fostering public policies, thus moving the score up from two to three (see the dashed-line boxes in figure 2-5).

With this information in her hands, Faith recalculated the scores and dollar amounts and made a final decision to locate the fund in Argentina, as you can see elaborated on in figure 2-5.

OBJECTIVES	SUB-OBJECTIVES	OBJECTIVES	
		Africa	Argentina
A. STAKEHOLDER PRIORITY ALIGNMENT (YES = 3; NO = 0)	Country's national aspirations matching	3	3
	Local Government supported	3	3
	Connection with subsidiaries' priorities	3	3
B. RIPE ECOSYSTEM IN CANDIDATE MARKETS (HIGH = 3; MEDIUM = 2; LOW = 1)	Abundance of candidate technology start-ups	2	2
	Academic environment with highly reputable universities	1	1
	Steady flow of new professionals coming from STEM courses	2	2
	Innovation fostering public policies in place	2	~~2~~ 3
	Mature intellectual property environment	1	1
	Identified partner in the financial system	~~2~~ 3	3
C. SELF-SUSTAINABLE	Existing foreign investment sources	$4M	$5M
	Available venture capital's seed money	$3M	$2M
	Available resources from local stakeholder	$150K	~~$1M~~ $2M
	Operational costs funding	$400K	~~$500K~~ $1.5M
	Committed funding from local partners	$1M	~~$500K~~ $1.5M
	TOTAL =	~~19~~ 20 and $8.55M	~~20~~ 21 and ~~$9M~~ $12M

Fig. 2-5. Trade-offs table for the creation of an emerging markets' innovation fund.

This is just one way to do it. The most important lesson here is that working with your stakeholders from the beginning, putting values to objectives, and sticking to an objective approach of "option evaluation" will help you make the best possible decision.

CHALLENGE 2-4: RISK MANAGEMENT

Establishing some sort of a process will help you keep consistency through changes. We talked about the need to step back and revaluate assumptions and actions constantly, and this movement can create instability. Using basic risk management concepts will help build a process that will keep you on track during your Solution-Design journey.

There are several risk management methodologies available, with a variety of tools from simple tables to sophisticated mathematical risk assessment models. We will present basic concepts based on definitions provided by the Committee of Sponsoring Organizations of the Treadway Commission (COSO). COSO is a joint initiative of five private sector organizations in the financial, accounting, and auditing fields, dedicated to providing leadership through the development of frameworks on enterprise risk management.

> The most important lesson here is that working with your stakeholders from the beginning, putting values to objectives, and sticking to an objective approach of "option evaluation" will help you make the best possible decision.

The general definition commonly found in dictionaries for "risk" is "potential exposure to danger or loss." By definition, there is an expectation that something will be negatively impacted. You want to obtain enough information to plan actions that could avoid this "something" from happening, or to minimize the impact in case this "something" does happen. This is a very simple way to define risk management.

When you are tasked with designing a solution for a complex problem, in addition to breaking your problem into smaller ones, setting up your objectives, and assessing your options, you can gather and organize information around the smaller problems in a way that anticipates the likelihood of something negatively impacting your objectives. A straightforward way to visualize the prioritization of your actions is a chart similar to the one we introduced in chapter 1, challenge 1-4, only now we are assessing impact vs. likelihood (see figure 2-6).

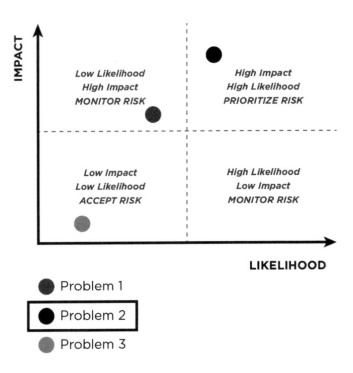

Fig. 2-6. Impact versus likelihood.

The problem you need to prioritize is the one with the highest impact and highest likelihood of materialization. With the ones where only one of those factors is high, you may decide not to do anything about it right then but to keep an eye on them. And with the ones where both impact and likelihood are low, you might just accept the risk. This is based on risk management principles.

Let's analyze another situation faced by David Lewis, the protagonist in case study 1-1, and use it to illustrate a practical use of risk management concepts.

CASE STUDY 2-4: APPLYING RISK MANAGEMENT CONCEPTS

As part of his plan to revamp the overall supplier management practices for his company, David Lewis decided to design a solution to implement a more-efficient way of prioritizing contract reviews. When he began, he learned that the team was only using the spend component to select the contracts they wanted to review. Every year, three months before the end of the fiscal year, the team would check the top thirty suppliers with the largest spend, and those were the ones they selected for a review. Some of them were reviewed every single year, and most of them were providing low-risk, high-volume services. David decided to prioritize this project when he found out that the power service provider was making the list every year, although it was not in the strategic supplier list (low contractual risk). In the same fashion, some consulting and legal firms that supported strategic and sensitive initiatives were never reviewed.

David started by creating a risk profile category he called "services," defined by the primary line of services each supplier provided to his company. He had learned through his professional experience that suppliers providing outside legal counsel or travel services deserved stricter levels of contract management reviews than the local power company did. Then he listed additional risk profile categories: "financial risk," "privacy and information security risk," "regulatory risk," "location risk," and "exit strategy risk" (see figure 2-7).

DAVID LEWIS'S SUPPLIER RISK ASSESSMENT

RISK PROFILE CATEGORY	DEFINITION
SERVICES	Main category spend, defining the primary line of service/goods provided (e.g., professional services, marketing, etc.)
FINANCIAL	Financial indicators of supplier's financial health
PRIVACY & INFOSEC	Level of supplier access to personal data, requiring additional information security controls (including certifications)
REGULATORY	Special regulatory requirements impacting the nature of engagement
LOCATION	Determined by supplier's physical (likelihood of natural disasters) or geopolitical (country corruption index) location
EXIT STRATEGY	Level of dependence on supplier (how quickly the company can move to another supplier, with minimum impact, in case of engagement termination)

Fig. 2-7. David Lewis's supplier risk assessment categories defined.

Once David established the risk profile categories, he attributed criteria to each category (see figure 2-8).

DAVID LEWIS'S SUPPLIER RISK ASSESSMENT CRITERIA

RISK PROFILE CATEGORY	1	2	3
SERVICE	Low-risk spend category	Medium-risk spend category	High-risk spend category
FINANCIAL	Low financial risk	Medium financial risk	High financial risk
PRIVACY & INFOSEC	Not handling sensitive information	Potentially handling sensitive information	Dealing with sensitive information
REGULATORY	Not impacted by regulatory requirements	Potentially impacted by regulatory requirements	Impacted by regulatory requirements
LOCATION	Not affected by location or located in a low risk site	Located in a medium risk site	Located in a high-risk site
EXIT STRATEGY	Can be replaced immediately and with no impact or low impact to business	Takes up to six months to transition, with low to medium impact to business	Requires more than six months for the transition, with medium to high impact to business

Fig. 2-8. David Lewis's supplier risk assessment criteria.

After applying the risk profile criteria, David attributed weights to calculate each supplier's inherent risk (IR), which is the risk associated to the engagement with the supplier before considering any controls in place—a contract, for example (see figure 2-9). David learned this from the COSO's May 2013 study "Internal Controls–Integrated Framework," which states that inherent risk is the "risk to the achievement of entity objectives in the absence of any actions management might take to alter either the risk's likelihood or impact."

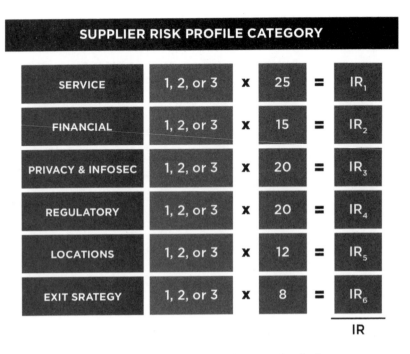

Fig. 2-9. David Lewis's supplier's inherent risk calculation.

David then built a risk framework to be applied to each supplier's IR, following the calculation (minimum and maximum values obtained when you apply the weight to the risk profile category values attributed in the previous table):

IR (Inherent Risk) between 0.6 (Low) and 1.8 (High)

Fig. 2-10. David Lewis's supplier risk assessment calculation criteria.

Finally, by ranking suppliers' IR (applying the calculated IR to the criteria), David got what would be the contract review cycle for all of the suppliers in the company's database (see figure 2-11).

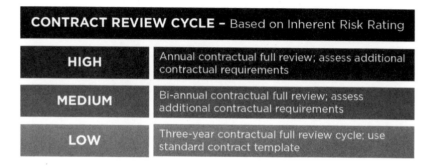

Fig. 2-11. David Lewis's supplier risk assessment versus contract review cycle.

In summary, David was able to use basic risk management principles to design a solution by building a framework that could demonstrate to his management team—and to his auditors—that there was a consistent contract review process in place.

KEY TIPS FOR CHAPTER TWO:

1. Define your objectives and get all your stakeholders on the same page.

2. Assess your options—map them, assign weighting, and negotiate trade-offs.

3. Use a verifiable approach to bet on the best solution.

4. Use risk management concepts to support your prioritization assessment and keep an eye on additional options.

THREE

ENGAGE

**Prepare Your Stakeholder Engagement Plan
and Influence the Decision-Making Process**

"Alone we can do so little; together we can do so much."

—Helen Keller

We believe that any successful Solution-Design process must rely on a carefully crafted Stakeholder Engagement Plan. What do we mean by this? A Stakeholder Engagement Plan is a series of steps used to clearly identify whom will be impacted by your recommended solution, either positively or negatively, and how to handle stakeholder reactions. To understand the impact and the respective mitigation measures, you will need to assess the stakeholders' level of interest in the decision(s) to be made, their respective motivations, and any personal feelings these stakeholders might develop when faced by the effects of your recommended solution.

In this way, you will be well-prepared to negotiate with them. These are additional steps that even experienced Solution Designers often overlook. This chapter will focus on how to do this by driving two key actions: (1) preparing your Stakeholder Engagement Plan, and (2) influencing the decision-making process

In preparing your Stakeholder Engagement Plan, you will learn techniques to identify and assess who the stakeholders are (i.e., stakeholder analysis), how to plan your interactions with them, and what steps you should take to better negotiate the approval of your recommended solution. Implementing these steps will increase your chances of resolving the essential problem.

Finally, you will discover why great Solution Designers share with others the credit they receive for their successfully implemented recommendations—another step often overlooked even by the most experienced professionals.

CHALLENGE 3-1: KNOW YOUR CLIENT

In this initial stage of the Solution-Design process, it is time to delve deeper into identifying and assessing the people involved in the decision-making and solution-implementation process. These people are called stakeholders, people who are involved in or are affected by your Solution-Design process.

Why is this so important? Because time and other resources might be such a constraint that you will need to prioritize which stakeholders will require more of your attention, what actions you will need to take to get them on your side, and the degree of urgency you will need to apply to the latter.

Begin by building a table or chart with your stakeholders' names, their position in the organizational chart, and their roles and responsibilities. Then add your assessment of their level of support for your recommended solution.

This initial stakeholder mapping and respective assessment is called stakeholder analysis, a series of steps to identify who your stakeholders are—whether they oppose or support your recommended solution—and what roles they play in the approval process. This process will become clear in case study 3-1.

Following your initial analysis, it's also important to acknowledge that these stakeholders might have a range of concerns about your recommended solution, which could be caused by often-unvoiced individual motivations. Equally critical, stakeholders have varying levels of interest in participating, as well as the power to intervene in the decision-making process.

Good Solution Designers carefully map out their recommended solution's stakeholders, and thoroughly identify their objections as well as their individual motivations to support or oppose each recommended solution. However, *great* Solution Designers go beyond that, taking the extra time to decipher each stakeholder's level of interest in the decision-making process, carefully assessing which stakeholders have the power to influence it.

Objections are concerns that stakeholders have with your recommended solution and its potential impact on them, the project goals, the financials, or the regulatory mandates. Objections are usually easier to understand, and tend to be based on technical or quantitative reasons. Motivations might not be directly related to the decision-making, and are more likely to be based on experience, empathy, or individual preferences.

To get to the "why" behind each stakeholder's position, you will need to weigh their objections and motivations against your solution. This can be achieved by building a table where you can add columns to include how to handle the objections with specific responses, and match the motivations with an explanation of your solution's value proposition, as in figure 3-1.

GOAL		REACTION		ACTION
OBJECTION HANDLING	➡	ACKNOWLEDGE	➡	RESPOND
		Show genuine empathy regarding the voiced objection		with specific actions to address the objection
MOTIVATION MATCHING	➡	CONFIRM	➡	EXPLAIN
		if your listening matches the actual motivation, sometimes unvoiced		how your solution's value proposition matches the stakeholder's motivation

Fig. 3-1. Stakeholder mapping—handling objections and motivation.

Again, because time and other resources might be a factor in your Solution-Design process, you will need to prioritize which stakeholders should receive the bulk of your attention, what actions you may need to take to get them on your side, and the degree of urgency you may need to do so.

Now it is time to add additional criteria to your stakeholder mapping, including:

- Power (high, medium, low): How able is the stakeholder to influence the decision-making process?

- Interest (high, medium, low): How interested is the stakeholder in becoming involved in the decision-making process?

You could even build graphs with action quadrants in order to have a visual perspective of where to position your stakeholders. In this case, you might want to simplify the values to "high" and "low" (see figure 3-2).

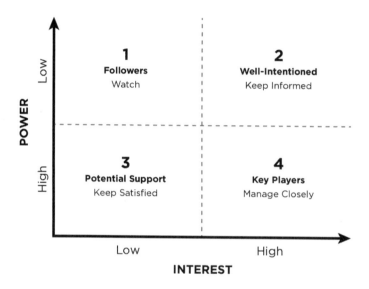

Fig. 3-2. Stakeholder mapping—power versus interest assessment. (Adapted from Mendelow's Power-Interest Grid.)[8]

This brings us to the next step. In order to conserve time in the process, you will need to prioritize who gets more quality attention. For example, stakeholders in the quadrant "manage closely" should receive more attention, because their support can ensure project success or failure, depending on how you manage them. This will ultimately constitute your Stakeholder Engagement Plan.

---

8   Aubrey L. Mendelow, "Mendelow's Power-Interest Grid," Kent State University, Ohio: (1961).

Planning and interacting in a timely manner with your stakeholders is key, and might even seem an obvious step; however, experience shows that the excitement of the Solution-Design process usually tramples it.

Case study 3-1 illustrates how to carry out these actions to ensure you create a successful Stakeholder Engagement Plan.

CASE STUDY 3-1: WHO ARE THE DRIVING FORCES BEHIND THE CRITICAL DECISIONS?

Devon Thompson, a project manager at a consulting firm, was tasked to help get clean water to Jamii, a community in Africa's countryside. His challenge? He must work with what is called a "collaborative arrangement." In this type of arrangement, no one owns the problem or the solution alone. It is a public-private partnership, with people who have diverse backgrounds and sometimes conflicting interests, but a shared cause. Devon identified representatives from regional as well as local nongovernment organizations (NGOs), the government, community, and the private sector, including small companies as well as large corporations.

To simplify, let's focus on the stakeholders that work for Devon's client, the Global Sunrise Foundation (a fictitious entity used for educational purposes only).

The complex problem the foundation faces is the lack of clean water in the rural village of Jamii, a poor community stricken by a severe drought for the last several years. No single organization is accountable for the issue, and neither can one tackle it alone.

Working with its partners in the collaborative arrangement, the foundation leadership has concluded that the best solution is to drill an artesian well with publicly known technology, sound technical procedures, and experienced people.

The options to get this done were set by the foundation as the following:

a. Subcontract with a regional NGO that has experience in Africa.

b. Contract with an international private contractor known for similar projects.

c. Devon's recommended option/solution: Transfer funding to Maji Safi, a local NGO that has previous experience in Jamii, although no experience with drilling large artesian wells. For that, the NGO would drill the well after training and accrediting its team, and developing local capabilities for any further well drilling

Devon started by identifying the stakeholders in the foundation, creating a table with their names and positions in the organization, and assessing their level of support (positive, neutral, negative). He also added the roles they play in the decision-making process or solution implementation (in this case "final sign-off," "recommends solution," and "subject matter expert" [SME]).

To find the stakeholder names and roles, Devon could either call the entities' offices directly, or read the organizational charts in the publicly published reports. How can he learn if a given stakeholder supports or opposes his recommendation? He could speak directly to them or to someone with access to them. Devon could also use public information found on the Internet, such as LinkedIn, to learn more about the foundation's stakeholder profiles, opinions, and previous experience with similar decisions.

Let's take a look at Devon's resulting stakeholder identification and support table, which will be built upon throughout his process.

- **Client**: Golden Sunrise Foundation

- **Problem**: Lack of clean water in native community, Jamii, Africa

- **Solution**: Install an artesian well.

- **Options**: (a) Subcontract regional NGO, (b) fund international organization, or, (c) Devon's recommended solution: transfer funding to a local NGO, after training and accrediting its team.

NAME	POSITION	ROLE	SUPPORT LEVEL
Liliana Medrado	VP of Operations	final sign-off	positive
Kat Nyati	GM of Projects	recommends solutions	neutral
Joe Ramos	Senior Geologist	SME	negative

Fig. 3-3. Stakeholder mapping—identification and support level.

Getting clean water to Jamii is a shared goal for the collaborative arrangement partners, and the foundations' goal is to deliver on it, but the way to get there differs from stakeholder to stakeholder. Because Devon has multiple options, and he is recommending a specific one, he will need to identify who is on his side and who is not. This way, he may be able to nudge some of the stakeholders into supporting him while neutralizing others who don't.

Next, let's understand the "why" behind the reasons a stakeholder might support or oppose Devon's recommended solution by understanding their objections and unvoiced motivations.

Remember, Devon has carried out an initial stakeholder mapping for each of the parties involved so that he could increase his chances of getting his recommendations on how to get clean water to Jamii approved. As we did earlier in this case study, let's focus on the stakeholders that work for Devon's client, Global Sunrise Foundation.

Devon created a table for handling the different objections and motivations of stakeholders (see figure 3-4).

NAME	POSITION	ROLE	SUPPORT	OBJECTIONS	ACTIONS	MOTIVATIONS	EXPLANATIONS
Liliana Medrado	VP of Operations	final sign-off	positive	Not sure the local NGO has the skills to do it	Offer an independent NGO's skills assessment	Deeply committed to helping the kids in the local communities—Ms. Medrado is not aware of the solution's connection to it	Showcase how the local NGO will also benefit the local community kids
Kat Nyati	GM of Projects	recommends solutions	neutral	Sees all options with the same weighting	Clarify your recommendation's value proposition	To get more skilled professionals in the community's region—Ms. Nyati is willing to hear new suggestions about it	Show that the train-the-trainer instructors in your recommended solution will also train additional local professionals
Joe Ramos	Senior Geologist	SME	negative	Does not believe a local or regional team can do it; led a failed well drilling project last year	Share case studies from successful well drilling projects done by locally trained community members	A very technical, leader of a professional association focused on geological research, Mr. Ramos does not trust regional and local professionals	Connect Mr. Ramos with technical professionals you know in the association who can vouch for your solution and the local professionals

Fig. 3-4. Stakeholder mapping for Devon's firm stakeholders—handling of objections and motivations.

This table will next be used by Devon to carry out his stakeholder analysis, which starts with ordering his stakeholders by their impact on the actual decision-making as well as by the impact the decision-making will have on them.

This ordering process is also known as "stack ranking," because you put the stakeholders with a similar profile in stacks, like "supports," "opposes," "signs-off," etc. The stacking is used to plan the amount of time you will need to spend with each stakeholder in your efforts to influence the decision-making process.

Next Devon must plan his interactions with his stakeholders, creating the so-called Stakeholder Engagement Plan.

As you can see in figure 3-5, Liliana Medrado, VP of Operations, holds the final sign-off authority on Devon's deliverables. After observing his stakeholders' objections and motivations, and understanding how the power was distributed along with organizational chart, Devon put together figure 3-5—a power grid and action quadrant to further his stakeholder mapping.

In Devon's assessment, Ms. Medrado had high power in the decision-making process as well as high interest, making her a key player. Therefore, Ms. Medrado falls into the "manage closely" quadrant in the power vs. interest grid. Devon will need to spend more time with her, carefully revisiting her motivations and objections, establishing regular communications, and spotting any change in this assessment.

NAME	POSITION	ROLE	POWER	INTEREST	BUCKET	ACTION QUADRANT
Liliana Medrado	VP of Operations	Final sign-off	High	High	Key player	Manage closely
Kat Nyati	GM of Projects	Recommends solutions	Low	Low	Follower	Watch
Joe Ramos	Senior Geologist	SME	Low	High	Well-intentioned	Keep informed

Fig. 3-5. Stakeholder management for Devon's firm stakeholders—power grid and action quadrant.

However, when Devon assesses two other stakeholders, he notices they do not have neither the *power* to influence the decision-making process nor the *interest* in being part of it.

One of them is Kat Nyati, the GM of Projects, who does not require being closely managed by Devon, because she falls into the "watch" quadrant (high interest, but low power). The other stakeholder is Joe Ramos, the senior geologist and a subject matter expert (SME), with high interest, but with low power in the decision-making process. In his case, Devon ranked him as "keep informed" in the "Action" quadrant. This means Mr. Ramos will receive regular communications as part of the group cadence, but little face-to-face time will be focused on him.

Revisiting the table on the previous page (figure 3-5), Devon might want to rethink the initial action laid out to engage each stakeholder, because now the *power* to influence the decision-making is more clear.

Once you reach this point in your analysis, you are ready to lay out your Stakeholder Engagement Plan. The more power and interest your stakeholders have, the more focus you must assign to their objections and motivations. Remember, this Stakeholder Engagement Plan serves a purpose, which is to help approve your recommendation of a solution for a complex problem. The ultimate intention is to better serve your constituents. Therefore, pay attention to any bias when mapping, analyzing, and managing stakeholders. Avoid first impressions and keep digging to identify stated concerns and unvoiced motivations. Sometimes a previous bad experience can hinder your stakeholders' assessment of which is the best solution for the problem they face. It is up to you to bring your stakeholders together, clarify their doubts, and change their perceptions. In doing so, you can secure their support of your recommendation. But you will have to earn it; it is not just a given.

CHALLENGE 3-2: GET YOUR STAKEHOLDERS BEHIND YOUR RECOMMENDED SOLUTION

Selling your recommended solution to your stakeholders and decision-makers—i.e., getting their buy-in—is a common mistake inexperienced Solution Designers make. After all, nobody wants to be sold anything. Instead, they should follow the lead of great Solution Designers, those who are effective in getting stakeholders' commitments to their recommended solutions.

As you have learned, successful Solution Designers start with defining what they are trying to accomplish, which solution they want to see approved, and by whom. Then, they outline their options, visualize trade-offs and concessions, and define their limits. Finally, when they have all their options lined up and their strategy for negotiating with stakeholders prepared, then—and only then—do they pitch their recommended solution.

Like these experienced Solution Designers, in this stage you will need to capture your stakeholders' attention. You want them to be willing to commit to your recommendation because they *want* it, not because you are *selling* it to them. Remember, it is all about your stakeholders, their motivations, their excitement, and their concerns. You should capture everything in a fully baked Communications Plan. What is this?

A Communications Plan is what you will need to have in hand for engaging stakeholders and decision-makers. You'll use it to inform and, in some cases, influence their decision-making process. Here is a list of questions that should be considered when building the plan:

- How should you engage your stakeholders? With an in-person presentation? What kind of tool should be used? A flipchart, computer presentation slides, or even cartoon storyboards?

- Is the engagement online? E.g., via email or Skype?

- Are props or mock-ups needed to showcase the products being advertised?

- What is the message to each participant?

- What does the forecast question and answer look like?

- When should any of the participants go public?

- Who speaks on behalf of the Solution-Design team?

When you are influencing the decision-making process, be sure to show your stakeholders your appreciation of varying opinions, whether or not they agree with your recommendation. You want to influence people who are opposed to your recommendation to come along, even if it's later on, and feel part of the decision. The problem that usually occurs, especially in complex decision-making, is that you risk having winners and losers. But you don't want any of your decision-makers to feel that they are going to lose something because they are opposing your recommendation. Even worse, you don't want them to feel that they are going to have to go along because the group, or somebody higher up, decided to support you. If you can, you should help people learn how to compromise for the greater good.

As Robert Cialdini explains in his book, *Influence, Science and Practice*, these are feelings that are explored by what he calls "compliance experts," professionals who just want to manipulate people to "comply" with their demands. Our experience shows that this can backfire; after all, no one wants to feel manipulated.

Finally, you must be careful not to be overly excited about your own solutions. When that happens, you might overlook other people's great ideas. Many times, because it takes some effort to get to the much-needed stakeholder commitment, you may need to evolve your approach as initially unforeseen solutions become evident.

Let's consider another case study based on a real Solution-Design situation.

CASE STUDY 3-2: IN ROME, DO LIKE THE ROMANS, AND SPEAK THEIR LINGO

Lindsey Hall, a marketing manager in a company selling toothbrushes, must approve a marketing campaign she had designed for the company to fully recover from critically poor sales numbers.

After a thoughtful Solution-Design process, she came up with two winning recommended options, which she called option A and option B. These options resulted from a well-executed Stakeholder Engagement Plan. Now, Lindsey must work with these decision-makers to ensure that they go along with one or the other of the recommended solutions.

If you are in Lindsey's shoes, remember how important it is at this point to know who the stakeholders are—which ones are making the decision, and what their power is to influence it. In this case, among the stakeholders, the CFO, the CEO, and the Chief Marketing Officer (CMO) have the final word. You should remember that they all have individual motivations and concerns.

The CFO might be interested in saving money or cutting costs. The CEO might be interested in gaining share. The CMO might even have a personal motivation of wanting to win an award in Cannes this year. Therefore, you should have organizational as well as individual motivations well-mapped out before presenting the options you came up with. Make it personal and acknowledge stakeholder concerns and this will be a killer approach.

In this way, you can adapt your pitch to each decision-maker, acknowledging their motivation, concerns, and objections. For the CFO, you might go with, "You told me that controlling costs is very important to you because you saw marketing campaigns with skyrocketing costs in the past. This is how this recommended solution addresses that." Then, lay out how your recommended solution does just that. Even though the CFO might not initially agree with your recommended solution, because of her fearing of potential skyrocketing costs usually associated with any marketing campaign, you are acknowledging her concern by showing your recommendation and your strategy to keep costs in check.

Fortunately, Lindsey completed her stakeholder mapping early on, although it would be wise for her to revisit it again as she prepares for her presentation to the decision-makers. However, it is not just presenting her recommendations that matters. Lindsey also needs a thought-out Communications Plan (see challenge 3-2).

As an experienced Solution Designer, Lindsey knew that—independent of the company culture—what always works best, despite today's interconnected companies, is engaging one-on-one, face-to-face. Otherwise, she would be just another voice on a conference call.

Another factor Lindsey considered was her stakeholders' communications style, which may vary with seniority, nationality, geographic origin, and culture.

When engaging with her audience, she prepared to speak their language, use their jargon, and even dress in the same style of the people she needed on her side. She works for a young and very informal company; hence, she rarely dresses up at work. However, she dresses more formally when she meets the company's senior leadership team (SLT), which has a more formal dress code.

As in Lindsey's case, if you work for a traditional financial institution and are trying to get your recommended solution approved, do not show up at a board meeting wearing just a T-shirt and jeans, because you might provoke an immediate negative reaction from your audience. They might listen to you, but often without paying full attention because they're focused on your dress style, which is much different from theirs. Sure, it should not work this way—after all, content and competency should be enough to get stakeholders to decide in your favor—but the reality is sometimes the opposite. And if you are trying to get your audience's commitment, then you'd better pay attention to every detail that might help or hinder connecting to them on a personal level.

Although verbal communication is key to the plan, Lindsey was aware of the nonverbal, body-language component. This is especially true if she is dealing with not only multi-country, but multicultural organizations. Like she does, you need to know with whom you should be directly engaged, whose hands you should shake, and who you should keep your distance from. In some cultures, decision-makers might listen a lot and not show any reaction. You might interpret this to mean they are not supporting you, when in fact they are very interested in what you are presenting. It may just be that their rich-context culture that values a more formal personal engagement, and they are just taking all the information in before voicing an approval or concern. In cases where the cultural norm is to avoid public confrontation, the decision must happen without your presence. Therefore, it is vitally important to understand the cultural norms, the respective body language, and additional nonverbal signs that you might be receiving.

For understanding these kinds of situations, the book *Kiss, Bow, or Shake Hands* by Terri Morrison and Wayne Conaway is considered one of the most comprehensive references of its kind. It is a complete guide to international business protocol, covering more than sixty country profiles and containing invaluable information on how to properly handle common business interactions with respect, the correct level of formality, and an appreciation for different cultures.

Lindsey learned to not be discouraged when her solutions were not well received during the implementation of her communications plan. Instead, she went back to the drawing board to identify her supporters, understand what changed with the initial decision-makers, review what didn't work and why it didn't work, and revisit the communication process. Real-world problem solving is not something close-ended. A feedback loop in the communication process is essential to influence the implementation phase as well. This way, it's possible to identify the issues that led a solution to fail. A feedback loop allows you to go back and revisit assumptions and begin again. More on how to do this in chapter 5.

Next in her Solution-Design process, Lindsey studied which methods of communication her decision-makers preferred. Some liked to talk for hours. Others preferred getting straight to the point. Some wanted a short briefing before the meeting. Others wanted to spend some time creating a personal connection with Lindsey. For each presentation, she customized her pitch to match each of the decision-makers' profiles. This led to successful conclusions and her recommended solutions were approved.

CHALLENGE 3-3: INFLUENCE THE DECISION-MAKING PROCESS

As we have learned, it's critical to prepare for your engagement with your stakeholders and decision-makers by crafting a Stakeholder Engagement Plan.

With this plan in hand, you are ready to kick off your negotiations with your stakeholders and influence the decision-making process. What is the ultimate goal of influencing the decision-making? It is to convince the stakeholders who are making the decisions that your solution is the best possible solution.

The case study that follows (case study 3-3) will assist in offering a pragmatic understanding of how this develops in real life. The subject of decision-making influence is sometimes a controversial topic because it can give a negative connotation of manipulation. If you want to dig deeper on this thesis, we recommend the author Robert B. Cialdini, who has written extensively about decision-making influence.

An experimental social psychologist, Cialdini studied what he called the "psychology of compliance." To truly understand how persuasion works, he immersed himself in the world of "compliance" for nearly three years, taking jobs with sales people, fundraisers, and advertisers to observe persuasion in action. His goal was to identify the main techniques used by the persuaders. Cialdini found out that there are six essential influence principles. In his book, *Influence, Science and Practice*, he guides us through several real-world cases, helping us to understand why people make decisions to acquire something they are offered (e.g., your recommendation).

The six principles of influence are:

1. **The Rule of Reciprocation:** "We should try to repay in kind what another person has provided us."

2. **Commitment and Consistency:** "Once we make a choice or take a stand, we will encounter personal and interpersonal pressures to behave consistently with that commitment."

3. **Social Proof:** "We determine what is correct by finding out what other people think is correct."

4. **Liking:** "We most prefer to say yes to the requests of people we know and like."

5. **Authority:** "We have a deep-seated sense of duty to authority."

6. **Scarcity:** "Something is more valuable when it is less available."

Another key piece of learning acquired during the many years we have spent designing solutions for complex organizational problems is to *make the decision-maker accountable.* In other words, make it formal and put it in writing. Communicate it back to everybody, i.e., "This was the decision that was made because of *A, B,* and *C.* Therefore, this is the reason we reached this decision, and this is how we are going to execute it." Or, "Here is how we are going to measure success. Here's how we are going to control progress, and we will report back on a weekly/monthly/quarterly basis."

Additionally, you might want to include what is called a "dynamic decision-making review" trigger. For instance, you could say, "In six months, we will revisit this decision, and we will report back to see if this was the best decision or not based on this agreed-upon criteria X, Y, and Z that we are determining here," and put it in writing.

> Accountability is about clearly communicating to all of the decision makers what the pros and cons are for the decision, how you're going to measure it, what the deadlines are, and how and when you are going to revisit it.

Accountability is about clearly communicating to all of the decision-makers what the pros and cons are for the decision, how you're going to measure it, what the deadlines are, and how and when you are going to revisit it. This is another point in the Solution-Design process where technology can help—keeping communications digital helps drive accountability.

A notable book that covers measurement to drive account-ability while influencing deci-sion-making is *Influencer: The Power to Change Anything*. In it, the authors use very interesting examples that showcase how people change, how you can influence them to change, and which influence strategies you can use to help people change.

The book also teaches you how to use the Influencer Change Model to leverage the six sources of influence (see figure 3-6) and make change inevitable. This model is about changing behaviors to achieve measurable results.

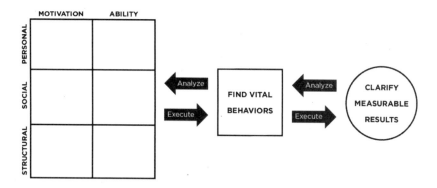

Fig. 3-6. (Influencer Change Model by Kerry Patterson, Joseph Grenny, David Maxfield, Ron McMillan, and Al Switzler.)[9]

Patterson et al. make the case that you change behavior by changing motivation and ability across personal, social, and structural aspects.

The main flow of steps is:

1.   Clarify measurable results (what you really want, time bound).

2.   Find vital behaviors (high-leverage actions that, if routinely enacted, will lead to the results you want).

3.   Use the six sources of influence (using the graph in figure 3-6) to combine personal, social, and structural sources with the motivation and ability domains)

---

9   Kerry Patterson, Joseph Grenny, David Maxfield, Ron McMillan, and Al Switzler, *Influencer: The Power to Change Anything*, McGraw-Hill: 2007.

In an interesting concept, Patterson et al. emphasize how critical it is to study "positive deviance," which means to delve deeply into the root causes of success or failure—specifically for those who succeed where most others fail—and find the exceptions. Then, you need to identify the vital behaviors behind it. For example, there might be people around you who stand out. If you look carefully and ask, "Who succeeds despite the odds?" and, "What do they do differently?" then you might end up understanding the vital behaviors that are behind success and failure.

It may take a while for stakeholders to make a decision, possibly because they have several great options, or because their individual interests conflict, or perhaps because they have little room for failure. Good Solution Designers listen to their audiences and acknowledge their interests. Great Solution Designers are able to help their audiences narrow down the options on the table and push for a decision within the existing deadlines.

As we have learned, decision-making influencing can be planned and structured by combining Cialdini's six principles with the Influencer Change Model found in the book, *Influencer: The Power to Change Anything*. The former teaches us that many decisions are made because of social pressure, or "conformity" with what is familiar, or sometimes even due to a sense of scarcity—real or induced. The latter shows us—as seen in *Influencer*—that effective results are measurable, time-bound, and address what you want to influence. It also highlights how critical is to work with your stakeholders on both their *motivation* (because they want to) and *ability* (because they can) to ensure that sustainable solutions are adopted. Once again, influencing is about uncovering a stakeholder's interests and motivations.

Let's see how a real-world case develops.

CASE STUDY 3-3: MEASUREMENT AND COMMITMENT DRIVE VITAL BEHAVIORS

For more than thirty years, Lightning, Inc., a family-owned indus-trial parts manufacturing plant, successfully grew at double-digit rates. Part of this steady growth could be attributed to a well-struc-tured recruitment and selection process, which had ensured that new positions were fulfilled with great talent at the right times. Unfor-tunately, due to dramatic cost-cutting measures adopted during the 2008 economic crisis, the company opted for fully-outsourcing both phases of the external candidates' recruiting process: sourcing and screening. This helped it go through those years with a new reality of fewer customers, lower profit margins, and cost-driven decisions. Five years later, in spite of the slow economic recovery, the company resumed its previous growth rates. However, the steadily increasing fight for talent, driven by a fierce competition from other players in Lightning's area of expertise, now required the company to hire more quickly, with more quality, and with fewer mistakes. The recruit-ment and selection process must include a broader external candidate sourcing (e.g., social media), followed by reliable screening (e.g., use of business intelligence analytics), as key ingredients of talent acquisition.

As the new head of engineering, and the biggest customer of the Human Resources (HR) department, Beatris Guedes, was deeply committed to helping the company improve its failing HR practices. She started by clearly defining the complex problem to be solved: In the last several years, Human Resources had been witnessing a dramatic decrease in the number of available external candidates with the right skills to be interviewed for critical positions. The candidate pool had shrunk to unforeseen levels due to several factors, including the lesser number of STEM (science, engineering, technology, and mathematics) graduates in the United States year over year, the proliferation of competitors with aggressive recruiting campaigns, and the company's own outdated recruitment and selection process. In the case of the latter, part of the current process was fully outsourced, in which both sourcing and screening phases had no meaningful metrics, were cost-driven focused only, and received no feedback from neither candidates nor hiring managers.

Nevertheless, Beatris faced a yet bigger challenge: the company's leadership—still hurting from the financial crisis recovery pain—seemed resigned with the situation and not willing to make big waves, especially in the Human Resources department.

Additionally, Beatris wondered how she could help Lightning, Inc., to increase the size of its external candidate pool, improve the quality of it, and keep costs down.

She would need to influence her key stakeholders and convince them to review the current hiring policies, leading to the adoption of alternative hiring solutions.

The first thing Beatris did was map out the stakeholders. Among them, she had Lightning's decision-makers for the issue at hand: SLT members (e.g., the CFO), the head of Human Resources, and the Labor Union representative. Following knowledge gained from the book *Influencer: The Power to Change Anything*, Beatris started by working her way through the Six Sources Strategy Matrix. For that, she set sail to identify the personal motivations of her decision-makers.

Then, she interviewed candidates, hiring managers, and other stakeholders. Finally, she crafted options, found opinion leaders, and used them to back her recommendations.

Finally, using the same matrix, Beatris identified the structural motivation as well as the structural ability to get key recommendations for Lightning to implement and achieve an improved recruitment and selection process.

With this information in hand, she followed Cialdini's lessons and moved to designing ways to influence the decision-makers. She started by using **social proof**: "We determine what is correct by finding out what other people think is correct."

Beatris had found out in her field trips and several interviews that a few pieces of criteria spoke to the heart of the key decision-makers. Therefore, she based her recommended solution on metrics that reflected that criteria. That said, the following metrics comprised the elements of a stable solution for Lightning which meant they would ensure that a sustainable solution would be used to address the strategic challenge.

Taking another one of Cialdini's principles of influence (**scarcity**), she showed that the CFO would not be able to keep process costs down much longer, because outsourcing expenses had been steadily increasing for years. Therefore, her CFO must support new ways of increasing the external candidate pool's quality while keeping costs down. For example, new technologies, such as business intelligence, could help the company in the screening phase while keeping costs under control.

Another Cialdini principle (**commitment and consistency**) came in handy. In Beatris's field interviews, the head of HR insisted that Lightning's team members should not just observe the candidate pool shrinking, leaving HR to deal with it. It was crucial that all the management team members felt the same sense of urgency to ensure that the company realized the full potential of candidate sources, attracting new talent before the competition did. The point made to Beatris was that once the leadership made a choice, they would encounter personal and interpersonal pressures to behave consistently with that commitment.

With this information and these influencing strategies in hand, Beatris recommended focusing on three actions to broaden the candidate pool and increase its quality, while improving the overall process effectiveness:

1. Establish a mixed process with outsourced and in-house recruitment and selection. Partially revert the outsourcing done in 2008 and move some of the recruiting phases to an in-house organization (e.g., for positions deemed critical) and use internal teams for external candidate sourcing and screening. For the less-critical positions, keep the process as it was, but control it better through agreed-upon metrics and regular meetings with the subcontractor

2. Improve administrative effectiveness by revising subcontracting practices to include providers that employ technology-supported candidate sourcing and screening. Automated feedback should be gathered from candidates, hiring managers, and other stakeholders, feeding into the regular subcontracting process monitoring, to be established in the new model.

3. Use meaningful metrics to drive efficiency for both internal and outsourced operations. Reach an agreement with stakeholders and subcontractors on metrics, including speed, candidate pool quality, and yield ratio (e.g., number of hired candidates per total number of sourced candidates).

Finally, for the sake of ensuring the CFO's—one of the key decision-makers—buy-in, cost-control measures should be in place and follow-up meetings should be held on a quarterly basis for overall program progress monitoring. Results should be shared with the leadership, hiring managers, Human Resources management, the Labor Union, and subcontractor leadership. Transparency should be key to ensure that Lightning, Inc., has the best recruiting and selection process in place, attracting the best and the brightest, which would ensure that the company kept growing and kept ahead of the competition.

This is a clear example of how a good solution tackles both the motivation and ability domains by speaking to the heart of the stakeholders while driving the intended behavior with results measurement, deadlines, and a sense of urgency. And, as recommended by Cialdini, Beatris used a couple of his six principles to influence the decision-making process.

CHALLENGE 3-4: GIVE UP THE CREDIT

Now, it is time to reflect on an often-neglected topic: who gets the credit for the success achieved during the project planning, negotiation, approval, and implementation processes?

We've learned through our experiences that great Solution Designers share success credits with their stakeholders, and we've found out that this has been key to ensuring that solutions last longer.

Many times, you will need to give the credit to one or more of your stakeholders so that they can feel appreciated by being part of the successful solution implementation. While it might matter for someone to take the credit, it should *not* matter to the ones solving the problem through great Solution Design. Because when the whole team benefits from reaching the goal, you can be sure the solution will be sustainable, and each and every one will own it.

Also, success is interpreted differently depending on the company's culture or country. Sometimes it is just a slight difference, other times it is quite significant. If you're working with various countries and different cultures, for example, you need to be careful about how you present your solution.

For instance, in the book *Kiss, Bow, or Shake Hands* by Terri Morrison and Wayne Conaway, the authors cover the way in which success is celebrated in so-called "rich-context cultures," like in Asia and Latin America. In these places, success is not credited on an individual basis, but always as a group celebration. There is no lone star; it's not about finding a hero—it's about the group succeeding *together*, with members relying on each other. Therefore, sharing the credits of a successful solution might mean earning stakeholder trust, thus gaining their future support to approve additional recommendations down the road.

CASE STUDY 3-4: IT IS NOT ABOUT LONE STAR HEROES

Silvia Oak, an experienced Solution Designer, led a successful consulting project for a large corporation in Tokyo, Japan. Her recommended solution had been fully implemented and her firm gave her an award—she was recognized as Project Manager of the Year!

Because Silvia believed in sharing the credit with her counterpart in the Tokyo corporation, she secured a cover story with one of the leading publications in the United States to showcase the corporation's project leader, Satoshi Takahashi. He was a mid-forties manager with the Japanese client, possessed great people skills, and had been fundamental in getting the senior management's commitment to the recommended solution, stakeholder support, and proper resource allocation. Without Satoshi's contagious enthusiasm and smiling interventions, Silvia knew she could not have seen the project through.

Surprisingly, the day Silvia showed up with the publication's crew to interview Satoshi, he seemed deeply embarrassed. Silvia asked him why, to which he replied, very humbly, "I really appreciate this, but the success credits are not on me. It wouldn't be possible if I didn't have a good team."

Silvia felt bad, because she should have known better. She had been working with Japanese organizations for years, and had learned that it is always about group celebration, not individual rewarding. Immediately, Silvia responded by asking Satoshi to invite his team to be in the cover photograph. She also said, "I want to ensure that their hard work which led to this success is acknowledged, and so the story will be about how your team succeeded, and how important the role of teamwork was at the end." Satoshi and his team were happy because everybody had been included.

Satoshi's story and his request to share the credit with his team also applies to us, the Solution Designers. Instead of playing lone star heroes, why not share the credits of our success? Down the road, this might make it easier to get stakeholder buy-in.

At the end of the day, Solution Design and implementation is all about the stakeholders. It is also about cultural awareness. It is about listening rather than talking. It is about reading body language signs. It is about listening to the hidden clues in the cultural exchange.

Sure, a big part of this is gut feeling. This is important, but there are also best practices, which you can learn from others who trailed the same path before you. Learning from these practices is similar to the Confucius quotation we used in the introduction: "The worst way to learn is from your pain. The best way to learn is from somebody else's pain."

KEY TIPS FOR CHAPTER THREE:

1. Identify your key stakeholders, handle objections and match motivations, and assess the decision-making power grid.

2. Prepare your Communications Plan and get your stakeholders behind your recommended solution.

3. Inform and influence the decision-making process and make your decision-makers accountable for their decisions.

4. Give up the credit, respect cultural differences, and celebrate success the way your decision-makers understand it.

FOUR

ACT

**Drive Your Implementation Strategy
and Execute Your Governance Model**

"Action is the foundational key to all success."

—Pablo Picasso

N ow that you have engaged your stakeholders, influenced their decision making, and had your recommended solution approved (by hitting all checkpoints along the way), it's time to act on your solution implementation—which means you must create and drive a strategy to get it done.

In this chapter, you will learn what a successful implementation strategy looks like, and how to act on it. You will also examine some daunting statistics regarding failed implementations. We will share with you some lessons learned from mistakes made by well-intentioned Solution Designers, who have, nevertheless, lost their focus, not paying enough attention to this phase of the process or underestimating the importance of hiring a program manager to help with it.

In the case studies ahead, you will learn preventative actions you can take to avoid becoming part of those horror story statistics. You will also learn from successful Solution Designers who realized they needed additional help with implementation and governance and how they enlisted it.

In this chapter, we will show you how your approved solution should translate into a project, what an implementation looks like, and what a governance model is. This will ensure your solution is not only fully implemented, but that it achieves the intended results and that your organization realizes the positive impact you envisioned.

Unfortunately, some inexperienced Solution Designers do not prepare well for the day *after* the decision-makers approve their recommended solution. They forget that a beautifully designed solution must become an actual project and be implemented accordingly in order to get through the finish line and drive the promised results.

This is a critical checkpoint because a significant number of projects fail in the implementation process. According to Wrike's "Complete Collection of Project Management Statistics 2015," 43 percent of projects implemented were challenged (late, over budget, and/or with fewer than the required features and functions), and 18 percent simply failed (either cancelled prior to completion or delivered and never used).[10] In 2017, the Project Management Institute (PMI) reported that bad estimates, scope changes, and insufficient resources

---

10   Emily Boone, "Complete Collection of Project Management Statistics 2015," Wrike, (2015): https://www.wrike.com/blog/complete-collection-project-management-statistics-2015/.

were the main reasons that about one third or more of projects failed during implementation.[11]

Ideally, you will have envisioned the implementation of your solution early on while you were still assessing your candidate solutions (i.e., your options). At that time, you might have performed an initial option-implementation analysis, in which you considered the level of difficulty to implement each of your options. For that, you might have created a table where you weighed these options against the criteria you defined in order to identify which option would better solve the essential problem identified earlier. Figure 4-1 is an example of such a table.

OPTION IMPLEMENTATION: INITIAL ANALYSIS				
CRITERIA	A. KEEP STATUS QUO	B. OPTION B	C. OPTION C	D. OPTION D
1. Leadership Team supports it (Political feasibility)	X	X	X	X
2. Current staff can do it (Administrative feasibility)			X	
3. Bigger economic impact per/$ (efficiency)		X	X	
4. Quick wins identified (Immediacy)		X	X	X
5. Geographic distribution of benefited branches (equity)			X	X
			↑ Recommended Option	

Fig. 4-1. Option implementation analysis.

11 "Success Rates Rise: Transforming the High Cost of Low Performance," Project Management Institute, *Pulse of the Profession* (2017): https://www.pmi. org/learning/thought-leadership/pulse/pulse-of-the-profession-2017.

At the kickoff for the actual implementation, you should go back to your Solution Design notes and check to see if your initial assumptions were correct, making any needed adjustments (see case studies in this chapter to see how to do this). Then, after you have confirmed your initial assumptions, assess how current your initial Stakeholder Engagement Plan is (see example in figure 4-2).

STAKEHOLDER ENGAGEMENT PLAN

STAKEHOLDER vs. OPTION vs. LEVEL OF SUPPORT		A. STATUS QUO	B. OPTION B	C. OPTION C	D. OPTION D
	1. Mayor	Barely Supports	Barely Supports	Fairly Supports	Fairly Supports
	2. CFO	Fairly Supports	Barely Supports	Partially Supports	Fairly Supports
	3. Regulators	Fairly Supports	Fairly Supports	Fairly Supports	Barely Supports
	4. Unions	Fairly Supports	Partially Supports	Fairly Supports	Barely Supports
	5. Customers	Fairly Supports	Fairly Supports	Partially Supports	Fairly Supports
	6. Branch Leadership	Partially Supports	Barely Supports	Fairly Supports	Partially Supports
	7. Leadership Team	Partially Supports	Barely Supports	Fully Supports	Fairly Supports

↑ Stronger Option

● Fully Supports   ◖ Partially Supports   ▶ Fairly Supports   ▲ Barely Supports   ○ Not Applicable

Fig. 4-2. Stakeholder Engagement Plan

In figure 4-2, while negotiating with your stakeholders, you have captured the level of support expressed by each one, compared to each of your options. After you have assessed the information in the table, you selected the option that had higher levels of support (option C).

Remember, while negotiating with your stakeholders and informing their decision-making process, you need to keep your envisioned solution-implementation strategy in the back of your mind, even if it is still just a vision.

Again, now is the time to pause and check your initial assumptions, evaluating and updating your Stakeholder Engagement Plan as well. Some questions to ask yourself are: (1) Does the plan include all the key stakeholders? and (2) Are you seeing the level of support you expected? If not, then you need to ask: (1) Was the plan realistic? and (2) Do you need to change the plan?"

This way, the implementation process will be more smooth because you will know who is going to be influenced or affected by it. The "people component" should be considered front-and-center in any scenario throughout the Solution-Design process. Unfortunately, even good Solution Designers kick off the implementation phase without acknowledging which people are involved and who will be affected by it. You can, however, leverage lessons learned and therefore mitigate risks while building on your Solution Design strengths.

> The "people component" should be considered front-and-center in any scenario throughout the Solution-Design process.

CHALLENGE 4-1: SOLUTION IMPLEMENTATION STRATEGY AND PROJECT MANAGEMENT

Congratulations! You made it to implementation time. Watch out, though, because this is when Solution Designers tend to make one critical mistake. Feeling energized by the recent approval of their recommended solutions, they automatically change gears into implementation mode and assume they can do it all by themselves. After all, why not assume the implementation phase will follow the previous pattern of success?

The reality is that any solution implementation that becomes a little more complex should be treated as a *project*. The Project Management Institute (www.pmi.org) defines "project" as a "temporary endeavor undertaken to create a unique product, service, or result." It is temporary because it has a defined beginning and end in time, as well as a defined scope and resources. Its uniqueness is due to the fact that it is not a routine operation. Also, it has a specific set of operations designed to drive an organization toward a clear goal. In many cases, the project team is assembled with people who come from different parts of the organization, perhaps even from different regions or countries. That said, the PMI describes the project management function as "the application of knowledge, skills, tools, and techniques to project activities to meet the project requirements." The PMI has certification guidelines and directives clearly defined in their *Guide to the Project Management Body of Knowledge*. In this guide, the PMI breaks down project management processes into five phases:

1. **Initiation:** includes kickoff meetings, project team recruiting, and resource identification, among other activities

2. **Planning**: encompasses organizing and preparing for the execution, with detailed staffing specification, procurement activities, and the development of project plans

3. **Execution**: how the work to carry out the project will be done

4. **Monitoring and Control**: This phase's primary goal is to compare and verify deliverables against the project plan and the requirements.

5. **Closing**: This is a sometimes-neglected phase. Because the project team might have been temporarily assembled, the Project Manager will need to transfer staff, archive documents, complete follow up task lists, and formally report the project results to the project sponsor. Otherwise, the project might morph into something else and be kept on "execution mode" forever.

Project management can become a muddy process. Although it might be good for the Solution-Design professionals to get their hands dirty and dive into the implementation of their approved solutions, too much of this might get them stuck in the mud. To deal with this level of complexity, it is highly recommended that you, a Solution Designer, enlist the help of a Project Manager (PM) to lead your approved solution's implementation. These professionals might be part of an organization called the Project Management Office (PMO), which is focused on ensuring any solution is properly implemented by treating it as a project. PMs have a unique skill set, including communication, leadership, negotiation, and risk management.

You can see how these project phases develop and will learn some of the PM skills mentioned within the case studies in this chapter. In the first one, case study 4-1, it took some time for the Solution Designer to realize that a PM role was needed. Fortunately, as you will see, it was not too late for a PM role to be added.

CASE STUDY 4-1: EVERY JACK TO HIS TRADE

Mary Spaulding was an experienced Solution Designer working for Tech2NPower, a public-private partnership focused on helping youth succeed by enabling them to be hired for tech jobs. After the 2008 crisis, Tech2NPower started to see its resources dry up. Then, in 2010, when things started getting worse by the week, Mary was asked to identify the problem's root cause, come up with options, and reach a negotiated solution with stakeholders in order to bring the organization back into the black.

For several months, she worked hard, envisioning a clever solution to improve Tech2NPower's financial health. Mary helped her organization focus on the essential problem that was causing the financial bleed. She crafted options for the needed solution and got the stakeholders on her side. She worked on the solution implementation for the last quarter but, somehow, it was not working out.

Missed deadlines, new features added to the initial scope, and fading stakeholder commitment had been haunting Mary for weeks. She could not figure out what was wrong until she shared her pain with Jeremy Barns, a longtime friend, who was also working for Tech2NPower's PMO. Jeremy was careful in his assessment, but precisely pointed out that Mary urgently needed to add a PM to her team.

For the recruiting pledging to her VP, Jeremy helped Mary to write the job description, prepared her for the meeting with the VP, and offered to get candidate referrals for the position. Because Tech-2NPower was a lean organization, instead of hiring someone, Jeremy ended up being assigned to the role of PM to help Mary.

He started by sharing with her what the PMI is, how it sees implementation as part of a project, and how a project should be structured in the five phases (see above). Jeremy underscored that Mary's key pain point was due to issues with the monitoring and control phase. He would ensure that she could compare and verify deliverables against the project plan and requirements. In this way, the missed deadlines and the recurring changes in scope would be under control in no time. He also shared with Mary how he applied his PM skills, such as communication. In her case, Jeremy would help her reengage her stakeholders using a revised Stakeholder Engagement Plan.

Moreover, in Jeremy's assessment, Mary was facing a typical case of project "scope creep," which occurs when new features keep getting added to the initial scope. Using a simple table like figure 4-3, Jeremy assured Mary that she would be able to get it solved soon.

IN SCOPE	OUT OF SCOPE
Define options and approve a solution to bring Tech2NPower back into the black, including: • Identify the problem's root cause • Identify stakeholders • Approve solution with stakeholders • Identify needed resources • Implement agreed-upon solution until deadline	Implement additional project features such as: • Change of facilities • Fundraising • Curriculum review • Financial audit • Employer recruitment

Fig. 4-3. Project scope definition.

In the case of the missed deadlines, Jeremy put together a simple table with deliverables, owners, and dates, because Mary could not control who delayed what in one single place (see figure 4-4).

DELIVER-ABLE	OWNER	DEADLINE	SUCCESS MEASURES	STATUS	ACTIONS
Example: Cost-reduction plan	*Example:* CFO	*Example:* June 30, 2010	*Example:* Plan is approved by steering committee	*Example:* Delayed, but still recover-able	*Example:* Add staff to gather data from business units

4-4. Project progress monitoring.

Jeremy explained that additional categories could be added, like "priority," "escalation path" (in case of impasse), and "status trend" (if it seemed worse), but that the simpler the table the better, because Mary was about to change the relationship with her stakeholders, providing them with more-reliable results in exchange for their clear accountability. With these initial project management controls, Jeremy Barnes, Project Manager, helped Mary Martinez, Solution Designer, ensure that her approved solution was properly implemented. Project Managers have singular skills that make them the ideal resource to treat solution implementations. Thus, you should consider adding a PM to your own solution implementation as soon as possible.

CHALLENGE 4-2: SOLUTION IMPLEMENTATION AND COMMUNICATIONS

Let's assume you have enlisted a Project Manager to help you translate your approved solution into a project, and then support you by planning and executing an implementation strategy using a project management framework such as the *Project Management*

Body of Knowledge (PMBOK) from the Project Managers Institute.[12] This Project Manager must be as good a communicator as their peer Solution Designers—you. This is a critical success factor for smooth implementation, because experience shows that more than 70 percent of their time might be spent communicating with other people.

According to the PMI's PMBOK, communication is an essential skill that PMs bring to the solution-implementation phase. It is critical that your stakeholders receive and absorb the information you share and take actions based on that information. It is also important that they are able to provide feedback about the implementation process—a key component of this phase—to secure that the loop is closed. This guarantees that you are revising your assumptions as the implementation moves ahead.

To ensure a structured and effective communication process, you and your peer PM must build a Communications Plan, which includes audiences, types of messages, media to be used, frequency to communicate, and escalation path in case of a crisis. It also includes how to monitor the plan's effectiveness, corrective course of actions, and roles and responsibilities.

However, solutions fail in the implementation phase because they lack such a plan. In the case study below, we will see how an expert Solution Designer communicates to her audiences, including stakeholders and committees.

---

12   To learn more about the PMBOK and its applications and standards, please visit the PMI's website at www.pmi.org/pmbok-guide-standards.

CASE STUDY 4-2: COMMUNICATIONS, COMMUNICATIONS, COMMUNICATIONS

Kate Hernandez, the seasoned consultant from case study 1-4, is our star Solution Designer. In this example, she was hired by a large organization to drive the local implementation of a globally designed outsourcing solution, which would impact approximately fifty thousand employees and contractors, hundreds of vendors, and millions of customers across the globe.

It had taken the organization's leadership one year of Solution Designing followed by a complex decision-making process to arrive at this point. Now, it should take another two years in the solution implementation, affecting several countries with cultural differences and geographically specific regulatory requirements and teams working across multiple time zones.

First, Kate established a local steering committee with the key executives/decision-makers as members representing all impacted divisions, mirroring the Global Committee structure. Although she knew most of these leaders from previous Solution-Design engagements, Kate realized this was a much more complex situation, with uncertainties brought about by a globally managed project implementation and fears of potential layoffs—the ingredients for a damaging distrust build-up. Her gut feeling, coming from professional experience, kept telling her that this solution implementation required a different skillset, and that she should bring in someone trained and experienced with project management skills.

Kate got approval for the local steering committee to be supported by the global Project Management Office (PMO), which would be responsible for monitoring and tracking the milestones and constantly measuring results through established reporting processes.

One simple tool used in this monitoring process, the Risk Mitigation Progress Report, is shown in below in figure 4-5.

RISK MITIGATION MEASURES

RISK	MEASURE	STATUS
1. Regulatory hurdles	Get legal department clearance	●
2. Board not supportive of new markets	Vet new markets with advisory council before coming to the board	●
3. Cost overrun	Hold monthly meetings between PMO and CFO team	●
4. Branch Management's lack of visibility growth plan	Hold offsite event with branch management for information sharing and feedback gathering	●
5. Sales territory overlapping between Current Markets and New Markets	Hold formal handshaking meeting with sales senior leadership from all markets	○
● Done ● On track ● Attention ○ Action Required		

Fig. 4-5. Risk mitigation measures—progress report.

Because Kate and the PMO were addressing senior leadership—members of the steering committee—they needed to use something graphic, crisp with color-coding, and on one page. This way the implementation decision-makers would be able to make the call to keep executing the initial plan or adjusting it in a timely manner. Kate convinced everyone that the PMO's excellent Communication Plan was central to the project implementation success. In fact, it had been created even before the "go" decision, during the due diligence process. Since the Feasibility Study, which is an assessment of the practicality of a proposed project, internal and external audiences were constantly informed of the company's intention, as well as of any adjustments made due to new information in that phase.[13] Also, the Feasibility

---

13   "Feasibility Study," The Project Management Body of Knowledge, Project Initiation Phase, 5th ed.

Study team had clearly defined who should be in communication and who should be part of the decision-making process.

Once the project was a "go," the key thing for Kate was to find out how to build the local communications approach—what would be the appropriate method, knowing that outsourcing for the unions and employees meant layoffs? How would it be possible to communicate this gigantic initiative when all that people would hear was that the company might layoff thousands of people?

For the external Communication Plan, Kate's approach included a close connection with the company's top third parties (e.g., application development vendors), the unions, and the key regulatory authorities. This would ensure that the implementation team would get an early warning if these external stakeholders voiced any concerns so that they would have enough time for clarification or course correction. Kate also made sure that key employees as well as customers were heard. Besides the established methods for feedback, she used what is called back channeling—a process usually employed in diplomacy—where, beyond the formal diplomatic relationship between ambassadors, diplomats have their own eyes and ears on the ground, people who are part of the community, who can listen to unbiased feedback on the side of the formal dialogue. For example, in a trade agreement talk between two countries, both negotiating ambassadors also have people on the ground feeling out intentions, assessing the political environment, and checking on commitments.

In a similar way, the outsourcing project had employees that Kate and the implementation team relied on, who had the ears on the ground and listened to the unvoiced concerns that were not captured in the formal feedback channels. For example, Kate's pathfinders might be the only ones to hear, "This is not really good. Better to delay implementation for this company's division now, because they are in the middle of a huge negotiation with clients." Or, "The unions are getting really anxious because they are in the middle of an election themselves, and the opposing party is talking negatively about this outsourcing and potential layoffs." This is the type of information organizations typically never capture through formal channels during large, complex project implementations. However, in the informality of chats during coffee breaks or social events, it is possible to hear feedback that can be worthy of further consideration for the implementation decisions.

A Communications Plan captures all of the various communications, including what channels were used and with what level of frequency, and, for Kate, a Communications Plan was the source for a monthly executive summary shared with the steering committee, as you can see in figure 4-6.

ITEM	MESSAGE	AUDIENCE	MEDIUM	ACTION	OWNER	DATE
Outsource goals	Target results are to be met by the outsourcing	All internal	PMO newsletter	CIO communicates the project goals and elicits feedback	PM office	11/30/2011
Community engagement	Social impact is everybody's concern	Employee families, clients, unions	Targeted letter from the CEO	CEO acknowledges the outsourcing's social impact and opens doors for feedback	Steering committee	12/07/2011
Labor Union engagement	Our organization wants to deal with this hand-in-hand with the Unions	Labor union leadership	Targeted letter from the CEO	CEO empowers the VP of Labor Relations to deal with this critical item	Office of the CEO	12/15/2011

Fig. 4-6. Communications plan—monthly executive summary.

Due to Kate's focus on continuous and frank communications with key stakeholders, her implementation team could finalize the regional outsourcing without laying off anyone in her region. How were they able to accomplish that? In Kate's region, the back-channeling process uncovered employee feedback that there was a scarcity of highly-skilled employees who could speak more than one language, which is a necessity for a company with global operations. From the feedback received, Kate realized that the employees about to be laid off could just be moved out to the outsourcing vendors because they were already trained in the roles and spoke the required languages. The global contract with the winning outsourcing vendors allowed each region to negotiate local terms (mainly due to different local regulatory requirements), and Kate and her team could transfer the teams that would be laid off to the local operations of the winning outsourcers. It was a successful implementation and a smooth transition.

Kate's experience reminds us how implementing solutions affects people. Yet, how many times do we see "leaders" making decisions without any consideration for how people may be affected? And they fail because they often forget to consider the impact of the decision on employees, customers, partners, and community. If the affected people are not familiar with the solution, they cannot commit, and then your solution will not be a sustainable one.

CHALLENGE 4-3: GOVERNANCE MODEL AND COMMITTEES

When you are designing solutions for complex problems, the odds that you will need to implement several projects at the same time are high. That's because sustainable solutions are usually addressed by multiple projects, which means there are multiple stakeholders and multiple interests involved. Employing the Governance Model concept will help you to achieve and sustain the solutions' implementation goals. The Governance Model should be perceived as a robust, repeatable, and sustainable model for your organization to manage all problems and related solution implementations in the long run. The Governance Model is the mechanism for your organization to transparently live by its values and achieve its vision and mission.

There are a few frameworks available to help put together a Governance Model, and one often consulted is the Committee of Sponsoring Organizations (COSO) of the Treadway Commission's framework. Developed in 1992 for evaluating internal controls, this model has been adopted as the generally accepted framework for internal control and is widely recognized as the definitive standard for organizations to measure the effectiveness of their systems of internal control.[14] Initially defined as the "framework and guidance for enterprise risk management, internal control, and fraud deterrence," it can be extrapolated and adjusted for any governance framework.

We learned from COSO that governance starts with the organization's vision and mission, and it is about the structure in place to ensure they are achieved. One of the COSO's thought papers defines "governance" as the "act or process of providing oversight or authoritative direction or control," and concludes the definition discussion by stating that an effective governance ensures accountability, fairness, and transparency.[15] Frameworks are important when you establish a

---

14 Sharise Cruz, "What Are the Five Components of the COSO Framework?" KnowledgeLeader, (October 2016): http://info.knowledgeleader.com/bid/161685/what-are-the-five-components-of-the-coso-framework.

15 "Improving Organizational Performance and Governance: How the COSO Framework Can Help©" Committee of Sponsoring of Organizations of the Treadway Commission (COSO), 2014. All rights reserved. Used with permission.

Governance Model because it promotes transparency for how the organization keeps the balance between its objectives and performance goals across the hierarchical levels and division, observing its own values, mission, and vision.

> **Frameworks are important when you establish a Governance Model because it promotes transparency for how the organization keeps the balance between its objectives and performance goals across the hierarchical levels and division, observing its own values, mission, and vision.**

A key component of a Governance Model is the establishment of committees to promote transparency and ensure that all relevant parties have a voice, at the right level, on the organization's management practices.

Committees are composed of people representing different areas, usually with diverse backgrounds, that together can make an informed decision on behalf of the organization they represent or provide expert advice to another committee or executive in charge of the decision. An organization can accommodate several decision-making and working committees with well-defined roles and responsibilities for each one.

The first step in building a good Governance Model is to ensure that roles and responsibilities are very well defined, which means ensuring that everyone is aware of what they are supposed to do. A well-known methodology to assign these is the Responsibility Assignment Matrix from the Project Management Body of

Knowledge (PMBOK) Guide.[16] It is commonly used for project implementation or for mapping business processes that can also be extrapolated to a higher governance model discussion. There are several variations of how to use the matrix, but we will use the RACI method here to illustrate how to apply the concept. "RACI" is an acronym that stands for "responsible, accountable, consulted, and informed." A RACI chart is a matrix of all the activities or decision-making authorities undertaken in an organization set against all the people or roles:

Responsible: Those who perform the task or work that needs to be achieved.

Accountable: Those who approve assignments to the responsible parties and confirm when the work or task was achieved (signed-off on). A good RACI chart allows only one accountable party for the deliverable being analyzed.

Consulted: Those who have specific expertise and provide opinion for the task or work achievement.

Informed: Those who are impacted by the deliverable but don't necessarily provide any opinion.

Figure 4-7 is an example of a RACI chart applied to a company's process to approve a new employee program.

---

16 "9.1.2.1 Organization Charts and Position Descriptions," *A Guide to the Project Management Body of Knowledge,* 5th ed.

CREATING A CENTRAL TRAVEL PROGRAM FOR THE COMPANY - RACI

	Policy Creation/ Adjustments	Booking Tool Implementation	Integration with Payment System	Travel Reconciliation (Expense Report)
Executive Committee	A	C	C	I
Procurement Committee	R	A	I	C
IT Solutions Committee	R	R	R	I
Finance Department	C	C	A	I

Fig. 4-7. RACI chart.

In the example in figure 4-7, the main decision body is represented by the executive committee, composed of the organization's senior leaders who are *accountable* for signing-off on the new policy and adjusting the existing ones as needed, and who are *consulted* on the choices for the tool to be implemented for the travel booking process. This might be a license to use an existing tool, or a tool to be developed by company's IT department. The executive committee is also *consulted* on the integration with the payment systems, and is *informed* about travel reconciliations and expenses reports metrics.

The Procurement Committee is formed by Procurement, a few influential users across the company who have informed opinions on purchasing practices, and also by select third parties executing the services. In this case, the company's global travel agency was invited to be part of the discussion. This committee is *responsible* for executing the travel program according to the policies, *accountable* for choosing the right tool to support the program, *informed* on the system integration with payment systems, and *consulted* on the travel reconciliation/ expense reports.

The IT Solutions Committee is *responsible* for executing any implementation according to the policies, *accountable* for implementing the booking travel solution and for integrating it with the payment systems, and is *informed* about expense report metrics.

Finally, the finance department is *consulted* on policy creation and on the options for the travel booking tool (to ensure policy is aligned with company's financial obligations and to provide budget information). However, the department is also *accountable* for the tool integration with the payment systems (ensuring the solution allows the company to meet financial obligations), and must be *informed* on expense reports metrics.

A practical application of the COSO's "The Cube" framework used as a guideline to build a Governance Model is illustrated in the following case study, 4-3.

CASE STUDY 4-3: GOVERNANCE AND COMMITTEES

If we revisit Kate's case study, we can see how she organized her committee structure model using tips from the COSO framework.

A Global Committee, composed of key global executives, supported Kate's project. In order to implement the local steering committee with key executives/decision-makers as members representing all impacted divisions in her region, she intentionally suggested mirroring the Global Committee structure. Each global decision-makers' stream had their own regional committees, which oversaw regional decisions and worked as advisors to the Global Committee. They had the autonomy to make regional decisions and influence the global team; there were no imposed decisions.

If we think about the COSO's "The Cube," the domains should be replicated in all organizational levels to ensure alignment as such (see figure 4-8).

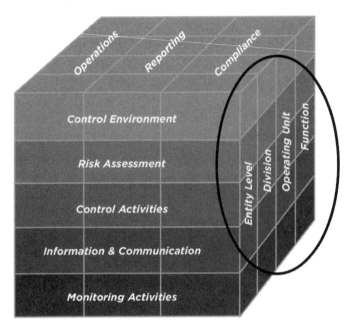

Fig. 4-8. The Cube.

Inspired by the COSO's 2013 framework (later versions may apply), Kate developed her own high-level framework that both global and local steering committees should adopt and regularly revisit (see figure 4-9).

FRAMEWORK FOR COMMITTEE'S COMPOSITION
(adapted from COSO©)

Committee members represent divisions in all the three pillars

Operations	Reporting	Compliance

And are committed to ensure the maintenance
of organization's Internal Controls

Internal Control's Principles

Control Environment	Organization demonstrates its commitment to integrity and ethical values, has established processes to ensure adequate management and an indetpendent board of directors, and promotes accountability for all individuals in the pursuits of organization's objectives.
Risk Assessment	Organization has a process to identify and manage risks to the achievement of its objectives.
Control Activities	Organization promotes control activities (policies, procedures, and tools) to mitigate identified risks to the achievement of its objectives.
Information and Communication	Organization promotes the functioning of its internal controls through maintaining adequate internal and external communication of relevant information.
Monitoring Activities	Organization promotes continuous evaluations to ensure framework's components are present and functioning, and that deficiencies are timely communicated and appropriately addressed.

Fig. 4-9. Kate's framework for committees' composition.

Each of the committees (global and local) were structured according to this framework (see figure 4-10).

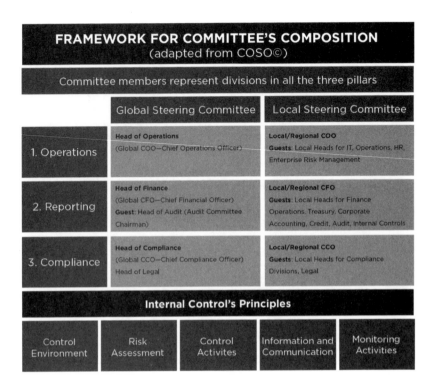

FRAMEWORK FOR COMMITTEE'S COMPOSITION
(adapted from COSO©)

Committee members represent divisions in all the three pillars

	Global Steering Committee	Local Steering Committee
1. Operations	Head of Operations (Global COO—Chief Operations Officer)	Local/Regional COO Guests: Local Heads for IT, Operations, HR, Enterprise Risk Management
2. Reporting	Head of Finance (Global CFO—Chief Financial Officer) Guest: Head of Audit (Audit Committee Chairman)	Local/Regional CFO Guests: Local Heads for Finance Operations, Treasury, Corporate Accounting, Credit, Audit, Internal Controls
3. Compliance	Head of Compliance (Global CCO—Chief Compliance Officer) Head of Legal	Local/Regional CCO Guests: Local Heads for Compliance Divisions, Legal

Internal Control's Principles

Control Environment	Risk Assessment	Control Activites	Information and Communication	Monitoring Activities

Fig. 4-10. Kate's framework implemented—inspired by COSO's 2013 "The Cube."

The use of a common framework helped Kate's organization to keep the committees aligned. It was then much easier to set up each committee's deliverables and align responsibilities between global and local committees, building up a true collaboration approach between both global and local strategies.

We cannot stress enough how important it is—especially in a multicultural, cross-border project—to consider the local flavor. Kate's project involved regions with completely different relationships to local unions and regulators. Her stakeholders had to be able to keep the focus on the common goal: the decision to outsource a non-core function, knowing that they had the ability to "localize" pieces of the plan, because respecting local nuances was part of the implementation Governance Model.

CHALLENGE 4-4: COMMITTEES AND HOW TO LEVERAGE THEM

Working with committees helps you to build your decision model based on aligning common objectives. Thus, it's important to understand the stakeholders—which in this case are the committee members. This is a structured way to ensure all relevant parties are represented and all voices are heard. For your organization, it is a way to demonstrate that these parties play an important role in a *transparent* decision-making process—and this is one of the most recurrent requirements of regulatory bodies across the globe. At this point, we'll discuss the different types of committees, how to leverage them, and how to engage with them.

Besides being the structured decision-making body, committees can also serve as informative forums, working to uncover information that will educate committee members tasked to make the decisions. This is what differentiates working committees from steering committees or boards of directors. Working committees have a more operational role, usually composed of senior managers overseeing processes and operational activities. They are closer to the "action." These committees can provide a detailed assessment for options to address the topics escalated to the steering committees or to boards of directors. These can include implementation timelines, resources needed, and impact analysis for each of the proposed solutions. Steering committees are composed of senior leaders who are accountable for driving resolutions, and who benefit from the details provided by the working committees to make an informed decision.

A common trap that organizations run into when working with committees for their decision-making process is the tendency to bring to the committees any and all questions received. Kate (from case studies 4-2 and 4-3) frequently received requests to bring issues to the steering committee's attention that should have actually been addressed at the management level. For example, she received an anonymous complaint about individuals with suppliers bidding for the outsourcing project that were directly contacting the organization's management team to brag about their competitive offer and get insider information to make it even more competitive. Although it looked serious enough, the company's code of conduct, which extended to the suppliers, already prohibited such practices and specified distinct penalties. A clear process for how to deal with such transgressions already existed. There was no need to bring the case to the steering committee. The employee assigned to manage the relationship with the involved supplier could address it directly, supported by the organization's code of conduct, and communicate the penalty to be applied.

You can drive effectiveness and efficiency by bringing to the committees only those questions that are not outlined in policies or procedures. In other words, those requiring further analysis and decisions that might be inconsistent due to variables that cannot be anticipated by standard policies and procedures (so-called "gray areas"). However, if you do need to bring an escalation to a committee's attention, then make sure your message is adequate for your audience. For example, if you are presenting your point to a working committee, you will need to be equipped with operational details. Working committee members tend to be closer to the operations. They will expect to have a more operational view from you. If your audience is the board of directors, or a steering committee, keep your message at the strategic level. Your audience will be more interested in an "impact vs. likelihood" analysis, preferably presented on one page with a simple chart.

The following graphs (figures 4-11 and 4-12) show a timeline with milestones, critical deliverables, and estimates, showcasing a Growth Project—code named "Polaris"—which was presented to the steering committee.

PROJECT POLARIS:
Growth Strategy & Next Steps with Milestones

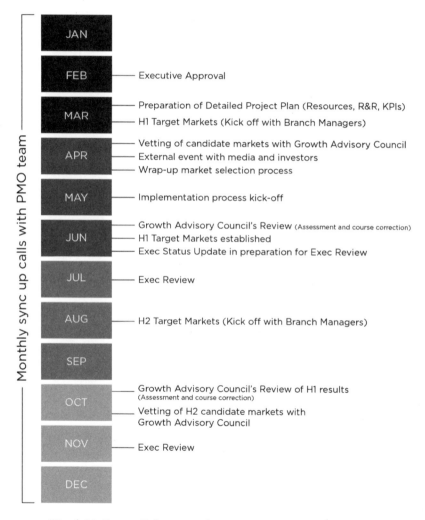

Fig. 4-11. Project Polaris growth strategy—steering committee.

The next graph (figure 4-12) represents similar information, but this time presented to the working committee.

Project Polaris:
Growth Strategy & Next Steps with Milestones

ACTION	OWNER	BY WHEN	STATUS
1. Executive approval • General timeline approved • Resources approved	PMO lead	February 10	●
2. Preparation of detailed project plan (resources, R&R, KPIs) • Plan presented to each workstream and sent to the Steering Committee to request additional feedback	PMO lead—each workstream lead	March 5	◉
3. H1 target markets (kick off with branch managers) • Identify key target markets per region	PMO lead—regional sales office	March 15	●
● Done ◉ On track ● Attention ○ Action Required			

Fig. 4-12. Project Polaris growth strategy—working committee.

In order to illustrate how important it is to adjust your communication to the right audience, you'll next review a case study where the advice was not taken when the team had to present to a steering committee.

CASE STUDY 4-4: SPEAKING IN TONGUES CONFUSES YOUR AUDIENCE

Lillian Hu, the Chief Information Security Officer (CISO) in a global telecommunications powerhouse, was set to present her recommended solution for secure communications to the company's board of shareholders. On her way to the meeting, she reflected on the task at hand.

Her organization had faced many leakages of sensitive information in the last several months. The last straw had been the publication of the latest plan to acquire one of the company's competitors, which ended up showcased on the front page of a major media outlet. After a thorough internal investigation, an external auditor identified the source of the leakage as a notebook that had gone to recycling without having the sensitive data fully deleted. Lillian was assigned to recommend a solution to lower the risk of this kind of threat happening again.

After assessing several options with her stakeholders, Lillian decided to recommend a solution that included encryption, a review of the IT recycling policy, and an employee awareness campaign. For the encryption part, she counted on Luigi Fioravanti's technical skills, one of her direct reports who was a young cyber security professional and a national expert in the field.

Lillian, a seasoned executive herself with years of experience designing effective solutions, was to present these options to senior management in a way that spoke to their hearts and minds. For this kind of audience, Lilian knew she must prepare very well for sharp questioning, thorough assessment, and sometimes a sequence of challenging questions—which tests the presenters' preparedness.

Lillian planned to meet Luigi in the conference room, and he had arrived early to ensure that the projector, slides, and the lighting were working perfectly. He was excited about the opportunity to join Lillian.

The board members arrived in small groups, coming in from another gathering. While Luigi waited, he became a little nervous, as the presentation was about to start and he had not heard from Lillian yet. She was known for her punctuality, so he assumed something must be wrong. That is when the board's assistant informed them that Lillian had been called away to an emergency at one of the company's branches. The CFO, to whom Lillian reported, had the option to postpone the presentation, but did not do so because she thought the leakage issue had been bothering the board long enough. With that, the CFO directed Luigi to proceed and replace Lillian as the presenter.

At first Luigi presented well, explaining the revamped IT recycling policy, the awareness campaign, and the respective benefits. The board rejoiced with the supporting data, the solution comparison with the market, and the estimated costs.

The presentation proceeded well until Luigi got to the encryption part of the discussion. He became overly confident with his performance, and this led him into a trap. When Luigi got to the encryption section, he started babbling about keys, the number of its bits, and the mathematical formulas behind each algorithm used in the recommended solution. He was so excited with his own knowledge that he did not notice the audience smiles morphing into questioning smirks, the sweat drops forming on the CFO's forehead, and the bleary eyes of the Chairman of the Board nervously squinting. It appeared that Luigi's performance was doomed, and he was the only one not realizing it. That's when destiny came to his rescue and Lillian opened the door, interrupting him.

Before Lillian could say anything, the Chairman said, "Lillian, it is clear you and Luigi know what you are doing. However, for the last third of the session no one could understand a bit of what Luigi was saying. Please, reschedule the presentation and come back prepared to speak in the mortal language!" Then he added, "You know that we are all committed to your recommended solution, we just need to absorb it, and this will not happen by talking to us about mathematical equations."

The situation created by Luigi's disconnection with his audience happens more frequently than you can imagine. Many times, excellent solutions are not approved because presenters are not prepared to speak the audience's language. When the audience is made up of board members, senior management, or non-experts, it is even more important to use clear pictorial exhibits with verifiable supporting data. Avoid speaking in tongues; skip using complex jargon and technical terms. Ensure that you connect with your audience by using a common language.

Incidentally, a month later, Lillian had Luigi present to the board the remaining third that was missing, and the recommended solution was fully approved. This time, however, he did not use a single mathematical equation.

KEY TIPS FOR CHAPTER FOUR:

1. Begin with a well-planned Solution Implementation Strategy as well as great project management.

2. Drive solution implementation on top of great communications and speak your audience's language.

3. Create a strong Governance Model and leverage known frameworks.

4. Engage committees and leverage them to support your solution-implementation.

FIVE

SUSTAIN

Leverage the Organizational Lifecycle and Create a Feedback Loop

"Feedback is the breakfast of champions."

—Ken Blanchard

Now that your solution has been approved and its implementation is underway, you might think that it is finally time to sit back and relax and let your stakeholders work it out while you savor the rewards that come with such successful experiences.

This is a common mistake that inexperienced Solution Designers make during implementation. But, in fact, more than ever, it is time to remain focused to make sure that your solution is sustainable. This means prioritizing resources as well as stakeholder engagement.

Otherwise, your entire effort may fail, reverting the whole situation back to the starting point when you had a complex problem to solve and needed to figure out which solution to implement.

Recognize that your achievements are the result of diligence and dedication. Throughout the design of your solution, you burned lots of energy convincing stakeholders, negotiating with hesitant parties, and reprioritizing scarce resources to ensure that your solution was successfully implemented. Moreover, the implementation phase may take months to conclude, even years, especially for large organizations with a global presence. To address this "solution-implementation fatigue," you must acknowledge that the business environment may also change. In truth, after a while, people tend to forget the initial compelling reasons for your solution to be implemented, stakeholders' enthusiasm recedes, and resources, including people, are redirected to newer, more-pressing issues due to organizational changes or brand-new complex problems that have arisen. Thus, for your solution to stick, you must be vigilant and keep those affected (including yourself) committed through to the end of the implementation phase.

Even when the conclusion of a given solution-implementation project is near, you still must assess what the next steps should be following the project wrap-up. This can contribute to the solution-implementation fatigue mentioned above—organizations have a lifecycle, changing dynamics along the way, and impacting the problems to which the solutions were initially designed.

CHALLENGE 5-1: BRIDGING OVER THE MOVING SANDS OF THE ORGANIZATIONAL LIFECYCLE

The best way to learn about organizational lifecycles and their perils is to turn to William Bridges, an author and consultant who has created a model to illustrate how organizations change over time. His model of the organizational lifecycle is helpful in preparing the organization's leadership to address the inherent issues of each phase of the lifecycle, dealing with the present while keeping an eye on the future. In figure 5-1 below, Bridges shows how companies start, mature, and reach a peak (phase 5: Becoming an Institution), before either retiring (phase 6b: Closing In, and 6c: Dying) or going for regeneration, starting anew at the beginning of a new cycle (phase 6a: the Path of Renewal, and 7a: Beginning Anew).

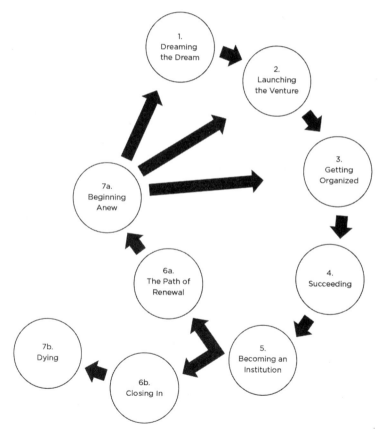

Fig. 5-1. Organizational Lifecycle by William Bridges.[17]

17   William Bridges, *Managing Transitions: Making the Most of Change*, De Capo Lifelong Books: 2009.

If your solution implementation happens while the organization enters phase 6a, Closing In, it begins to operate as if it were invulnerable to the challenges that gave rise to the company in the first place. Be careful here: according to Bridges, this stage marks the loss of the vital tension between the organization and its environment, degenerating into bureaucracy or simply losing its ability to sustain its success. This might mean that your stakeholders will not take risks or will lose interest in your success. In the case of a company merging, be prepared to capture any interim results in your original company that you could use in the resulting organization. This way, if your solution is still valid, it might be easier to get the new stakeholders committed to it. In a worst-case scenario, the organization may have no choice but to go straight to phase 7a, Dying, where it *will* eventually die. This means it may end up being sold or absorbed by another organization. And, in the worst possible outcome, it may simply shut down.

On the other hand, if your solution implementation happens while the organization enters phase 6b, the Path of Renewal, the organization may choose not to close in, but rather to renew itself. Bridges highlights that renewal comes not by fixing problems, nor by changing specific practices or cultural values, but by taking the organization back to the start of its lifecycle. In this case, the company will move to phase 7b, Beginning Anew. This will lead to going back to the beginning, re-dreaming, relaunching, and reorganizing in a purposeful transition into a new lifecycle. Bridges warns that this is not easy, since the organization might have developed systems to protect itself from the kind of change needed to move it back to the start of the life cycle. In case study 5-1 you'll see a real-world example of this situation.

CASE STUDY 5-1: EVOLVE OR DIE

The Eye on the Future: Research Initiative (EFRI) was created somewhere between ten and fifteen years ago after two leading technological organizations—with two different approaches for investigating new technologies—merged. There was reasoning behind the union. The resulting organization must keep an eye on the five-to-ten-year growth horizon, enabled by developing technologies, while the rest of the company focused on the one-to-three-year strategy execution horizon.

Unfortunately, with several leaders coming and going, and the resulting conflicts created by a merger between different cultures, the current scenario was ripe with undelivered promises, unmatched expectations, and generalized frustration. The initiative had lost its original focus and its goals were unclear. To make it worse, results were weak at best, and in some cases, nonexistent. Morale was low, and EFRI was losing key personnel every other month.

In 2016, Chuck Steady, the newly appointed Director of Applied Research at the company, was just beginning to grasp what he had inherited. The previous director had been poached by a competitor, and there was very little recorded history available to provide a baseline.

Chuck soon realized this was not the first time the company had tried to manage research of new technologies using a centralized approach. In 2010, recurring reorganizations of research teams led to lower morale, with many of its researchers leaving the company—the same problem they were now facing. Five years later, research moved from being a troublesome part of the organization to a company strength. All was going very well until the recent merger took place. Every gain earned in the last several years went out the window in the resulting organization. What concerned Chuck the most was that nobody seemed to realize that EFRI was stuck in time, hanging in the air. To him, it felt like the team members were just waiting for the unavoidable end.

Aware that organizations have a lifecycle of their own, Chuck decided to face head on the issues presented by the current phase where EFRI was stuck at: phase 5, Becoming an Institution. When an organization is at this phase, it becomes more interested in occupying territory than in conquering it. And it relies on the reputation it built over several years of success.

In his assessment of EFRI against Bridges's Organizational Lifecycle, Chuck identified additional typical characteristics, which are presented in the followed table (figure 5-2).

EFRI'S ASSESSMENT

- New researchers were chosen less for their talent or how *hungry* they were than for how they would fit in with the reigning mental model of "complacency"
- There was a sense of "having arrived" and no urgency about moving ahead
- How things were done had become more important than why they were done
- Existing norms were more important than listening to the outside world, and questioning them was taboo

Fig. 5-2. Organizational Lifecycle—phase 5: Becoming an Institution (Inspired by William Bridges.)[18]

As Chuck learned, according to Bridges from this point on, if nothing was done, the organization was in phases 6b and 6c, and was set to be retired. However, Chuck wanted a different path for

---

18   Ibid.

EFRI. He wanted to go for an organizational renewal—phases 6a and 7a—leveraging each group's strengths and streamlining cross-team communications to enable the company to focus on today's customer needs as well as on ones in the near future.

Chuck wondered, "Which should be the key steps to sustain and renew the company's commitment to EFRI?" He lacked an enthusiastic crowd supporting his pledge to revamp EFRI, so he needed to find ways to gather his stakeholders, and then together push for the much-needed renewal.

Chuck decided to "go to the balcony"—the concept taught in chapter 1. Using this approach, he stepped back—onto the balcony—and took a vantage point to assess the scenario—the dance floor—in front of him, and, from there, Chuck was able to reflect on what was happening. Coming back to the "dance floor," having realized that he needed to better engage his stakeholders, peers, and senior leadership, Chuck prepared a table reflecting his stakeholders' motivations and objections to support an organizational renewal or not.

Figure 5-3 is a sample of the results of Chuck's reflections from the balcony.

NAME	POSITION	ROLE	SUPPORT	OBJEC-TIONS	ACTION	MOTIVA-TION	ACTION
Lilibeth Stevens	Senior Researcher	Leader, EFRI's research community	Positive	Unsure about next steps, if any	Share the Organizational Lifecycle and the Path to Renewal option.	Committed to EFRI's success, wants to see the research community's opinion valued	Commit to clear options to highlight the community's contributions to the envisioned new (revamped) organization
Jasmine Aurora	Head of Project Management	SME	Neutral	Still waiting for definitions on what to implement, by when, and with which resources	Clarify the deliverables for the new organization's revamping	Wants to see her PMs involved from the beginning	Invite Mrs. Aurora to the Board of Directors defining the new organizational structure, therefore she can visualize her PMs connection
Pierre Lafont	Head of Product Development	End user of EFRI's research results	Negative	Skeptical of EFRI's revamping leading to delivering on his expectation of "killer" research results	Share the plans for the revamped organization	Mr. Lafont must clearly see the connection between applied research and product development.	Add Mr. Lafont to the Board of Directors defining the new organizational structure, therefore ensuring he can influence which research goals will be prioritized

Fig. 5-3. Reflections from the balcony—stakeholders versus objections and motivations.

Additionally, Chuck used the Five Whys technique to drill down on EFRI's essential problem. Chuck also revisited the organization's purpose by questioning it together with his stakeholders: "How could EFRI help the new company serve customers by researching new technologies?"

Chuck also understood that he must create a "holding environment" for people struggling with the new organization. This meant creating opportunities for EFRI's members to voice their concerns without fearing criticism or retribution. In cases like this, bringing in an external facilitator can help.

Most importantly, Chuck needed to give voice to the leadership on the ground floor, i.e., to the researchers still imbued with the original vision. He hoped that someone would listen to their feedback and input. This is fundamental to determining the timing of when to "go on the offense," meaning actively engaging audiences to share their visions of the "new beginning." Chuck had to rely on regularly reviewing the initial stakeholder mapping and prioritizing where to focus as the reality evolved.

In the end, Chuck offered his stakeholders a plan to recover EFRI's original mission, that plan would feature a key piece of the new solution for the company's need to anticipate any future technologies: Chuck created a feedback loop, similar to the Hollywood movie from the 1980s about going back to the past to impact the future. To ensure that he could realize his vision for a revamped EFRI organization, he created opportunities for small wins, avoiding what is known as "boiling the ocean," which is when managers try to solve all of their problems at once. Using this approach, Chuck identified opportunities to show progress in the short term and reinvigorate the realization of his vision, all the while working hard on the long-term goals.

An example of a small win was defining roles and responsibilities for each key stakeholder. Together, by qualifying the type of technologies that would be picked short-term, Chuck could give the group something easy to achieve and celebrate the milestone. The team started feeling as one, unified with a common purpose, which meant real progress.

After weeks of negotiation, checking back with his leadership, his team, and his stakeholders, Chuck finally realized his vision as his recommended solution was unanimously approved.

In this kind of situation, it is critical to identify the stage in which your organization belongs. For Chuck, EFRI had reached a peak. He was fortunate to clarify that, so that he could assess his options ahead more clearly. Then he communicated this to the group that they would either shut EFRI down or pursue its renewal, which he recommended. With good stakeholder engagement, Chuck brought everybody along, and his recommended solution was approved.

Now that he had the green light to revamp EFRI's charter and get the organization to start anew, it was time to plan the transition. It was finally time to move the teams into their New Reality, as coined by Bridges, which you will learn how to do in the next challenge and its respective case study.

CHALLENGE 5-2: GETTING THROUGH THE TRANSITION ZONES

Successful leaders should use a structured approach for managing changes and transition. One critical teaching in Bridges's book, *Managing Transitions: Making the Most of Change*, is about the difference between *changes* and *transitions*. While change might be situational and can happen without people transitioning, transition always affects them. According to the author, transition can be explained by a three-stage process, wherein team members gradually accept the details of the new situation and absorb the changes that accompany it.

1. **The Ending Zone**: This initial stage is about losing and letting go. Leaders must help their teams deal with tangible and intangible losses, preparing them to move on.

2. **The Neutral Zone**: This is a critical stage. Here, leaders must support their people getting through it. It is the right time to create incentives for innovative members who dare to take the leap, helping pitch the envisioned future as a growth opportunity.

3. **The New Beginning**: In this stage managers must focus on helping their team members nurture the organization's new identity, experiment with new opportunities, and realize the new sense of purpose carried out by the change.

Bridges also points out that before the transition kicks off, *certainty* is the general feeling among people. They are accustomed to the current situation, and many times do not even think of change until they face it. In cases of organization renewal, when transition affects people, some team members tend to reject the sometimes already occurring change.

Once the transition starts for real, *ambiguity* defines the Neutral Zone. It's a difficult situation for most people, because keeping the status quo is not an option anymore, and the envisioned ending—the future—is not clear yet. This zone needs extra caution, once you are neither focusing on the status quo (the past) nor on the new beginning (the future). Common feelings experienced between the Ending Zone and the Neutral Zone are denial, shock, anger, frustration, and stress. It is when many members end up leaving the organization, and when you are most vulnerable to losing key talent. The organization might not be able to afford to lose them without impacting the transition.

Otherwise, this might contribute to the organization getting stuck in the Neutral Zone for longer than planned.

From the Neutral Zone until the organization is finally able to enter the New Beginning Zone, members might voice feelings of skepticism, acceptance, hope, and enthusiasm.

Bridges recommends "interventions" to minimize negative feelings and leverage the positive ones, such as:

- mapping stakeholders and team members—identifying who will lose what

- holding regular team meetings—starting even before the change, and

- talking to employees, asking what problems they have with the change.

Additionally, it is key that the leadership is aware of common mistakes made during transitions. We have seen managers try to explain change via email while others used an organizational chart to lay out the future.

We were once given the impossible task to develop the entire transition plan alone, while our manager focused on something else. Some inexperienced managers make their team's life miserable by breaking up change into smaller stages, giving the impression of an endless transition. The worst mistake is to drive the transition by threatening reticent team members.

Fortunately, we have all experienced transitions led by real leadership. They create small wins, giving rewards to innovative team members. These leaders use ambiguity to continuously improve, create special events and logos for the New Beginning, and offer training to prepare for the new reality, many times using external speakers to motivate the group.

Transition experts know that leadership that communicates during transitions may be the differentiator between failure and success. Managers are encouraged not to rationalize bad news because the "factory floor" already has the news. Also, leaders must keep communicating, considering that it takes time for the news to sink in. Transitioning is about building trust—therefore say what you know, say what you don't know, and ask for time to bring back more information.

Finally, in your communications, respect the past; do not ridicule it. Position the past as a foundation for the envisioned new beginning.

> **Transitioning is about building trust—therefore say what you know, say what you don't know, and ask for time to bring back more information.**

CASE STUDY 5-2: HOW CHUCK USED TRANSITION ZONES TO SUPPORT EFRI'S TEAM

Using his initial work done in case study 5-1, Chuck decided to dig deeper into what Bridges teaches for successfully managing changes and transitions. Chuck used the concepts described therein to structure EFRI's transition to its new, revamped charter.

He started by preparing a graphic representation of the upcoming transition facing the EFRI team (see figure 5-4).

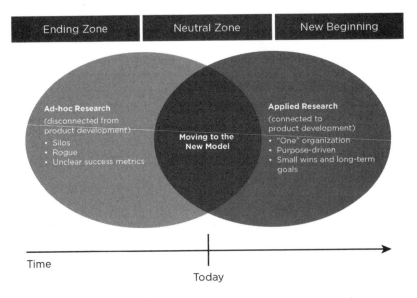

Fig. 5-4. Reflections from the balcony—stakeholders versus objections and motivations.

The critical issue faced by EFRI in the current situation, the so-called Ending Zone, was the disconnect between the new company's business goals (after the merge) and the research unit's charter. Working in silos, with no clear direction, and without crisp success metrics, EFRI was sometimes seen by the company's leadership as a rogue organization, operating independently and with no accountability. Hence, Chuck named this stage "Ad-hoc Research."

Chuck and his direct reports envisioned a New Beginning for EFRI, moving to a situation where the research unit would work closer to the business units, especially Product Development. Also, the research unit would pursue its original purpose of investigating new technologies that could impact the company's core business. Chuck named this "Applied Research." Finally, Chuck planned small wins and long-terms goals for the New Beginning, keeping the team's motivation even after ending the transition.

In between, Chuck drew a red area, the Neutral Zone, which he named "Moving to the New Model," to make it simple for his team. This was the zone where Chuck and his team would spend considerable time ensuring that the transition went as smoothly as possible.

Let's look at how Chuck addressed each of the transition stages, starting with the Ending Zone. He decided to focus on the specific psychological and organizational challenges that such a transition entails, helping his team navigate it through different stages of the change process. Michelle Baines, an expert facilitator, was hired to drive the conversation between Chuck and his leadership team. She started by writing a series of questions on the whiteboard during the kick off meeting:

- How happy is the team with the status quo? Why?
- What will change or need to change? Are there behaviors to be encouraged/discouraged?
- Is there a safe environment to capture the "floor feedback?"

After getting answers to those questions, Michelle directed the group on defining actions to encourage the *endings*. First of all, she asked the group to clearly describe the transition in as much detail as possible, identifying who had to let go of what and by when.

Intangible losses were added to the tangible losses, and were openly and sympathetically acknowledged. This was important, because loss is subjective, and the leadership agreement with it (or not) is irrelevant.

Turning to the Neutral Zone, the group covered the psychological aspects of this stage. Those included an increase in anxiety and a decrease in motivation that affects people in such a way that they become resentful and protective, self-doubting, and consequently less productive. Chuck and his direct reports were prepared for the chaotic times ahead of them. They were told to expect high turnover because several team members might react to mixed signals and confusion in this zone, leaving important tasks undone.

Michelle warned that people tend to take opposite stances, with some rushing forward while others hold back and hang on to the reality they are accustomed to. That is when the company becomes most vulnerable to the competition.

An important point raised by Michelle was the need to limit changes to the critical ones when going through the Neutral Zone. Teams can deal with reasonable change if they see it as a component of the announced one. Unfortunately, some managers use the transition to a new beginning as an excuse to introduce unrelated changes, and this can be a tipping point, causing unnecessary stress and triggering revolt. Instead, good transition managers plan for small wins so that people perceive they are making progress.

Moving to the New Beginnings phase, the team defined the vision for the change, clearly explaining the benefits and challenges of the new reality. The team members were given a role in the transition, as well as in the new reality.

The execution of the transition plan created with Michelle's help went well, however it wasn't easy to carry it out through the Neutral Zone. Some team members could not withstand the anxiety and uncertainty, and ended up leaving. Others found a fresh purpose in the new organization and played a crucial role as innovators. Chuck felt compelled to admonish a couple of employees at times, due to their absenteeism. He remembered Michelle's advice that he had to let it go.

A couple of months later, it was finally time to celebrate the new reality and close the transition from the Neutral Zone to the

New Beginning. Chuck directed his team to organize a big party to symbolize EFRI's new reality. The team created a logo for the new organization, there was a hackathon (an innovation competition), and rewards were given to the winners.

Aware that even at this stage there might be some hiccups and that a few team members might step back into old behaviors, Chuck kept up the transition board meetings for an additional quarter, ensuring that communications were flowing, and that subsequent celebrations were organized to commemorate anniversaries, small wins, and feedback from the factory floor (frontline employees).

The major lessons learned from Chuck were about consistency of communications, attention to the psychological aspects of the transition, and steady execution. Applying Chuck's experience is important in succeeding in driving your own transition.

CHALLENGE 5-3: RECOVERING FROM FAILURE AND LEARNING HOW TO SUCCEED FROM IT

It is easy to get distracted by the success of your initial implementation, missing the signs on the wall that alert you to changes in the supporting environment, shifts in stakeholder commitments, and the initial problem morphing out into something else, therefore invalidating the initially envisioned solution, and leading to overall failure.

It's more common than we'd like to acknowledge for Solution Designers *not* to spot failure in time to avoid it. Even worse than failing, many do not know how to use failure as a learning tool, and so they fail to correct the course, making their solutions unsustainable over time.

"Success comes through rapidly fixing our mistakes rather than getting things right first time," writes Tim Harford in his book,

Adapt: Why Success Always Starts with Failure.[19] He advocates that the world turned too complex and we must adapt, exploring options for turning failure into success.

Reading the above, most of us would agree with Harford. However, it does not seem to match our everyday reality. When people make mistakes, it is so upsetting that they tend to miss the key benefit of failing, which is learning from it, applying the lessons learned to fix any issues and succeeding the next time.

Moreover, in many organizations, management is still concerned with being perceived as lenient for tolerating failures, keeping their teams from taking risks and growing. Corroborating this, Amy Edmondson shared that most managers she encountered voiced concerns that an understanding response to failures would simply create a lax work environment in which mistakes would multiply. She advised that a new paradigm that recognizes the inevitability of failure in today's complex work organizations should be applied instead. After all, counters Amy, "those that catch, correct, and learn from failure before others do will succeed." She goes on to warn, "Those that wallow in the blame game will not."[20]

Ways to recover from failure when implementing solutions in multi-stakeholder environments include listening to stakeholders, feeling the authorizing environment, and framing challenges as opportunities. The authorizing environment assessment is important because it lays out who the decision-makers, influencers, and resource owners are.[21]

---

19   Tim Harford, *Adapt: Why Success Always Starts with Failure*, Picador, May 2012.

20   Amy Edmondson, "Strategies for Learning from Failure," *Harvard Business Review*, (April 2011): https://hbr.org/2011/04/strategies-for-learning-from-failure?referral=00060.

21   Patrick Dobel and Angela Day, "A Note on Mapping: Understanding Who Can Influence Your Success," Evans School of Public Affairs, Electronic Hallway, (2005): http://ambounds.org/docs/334/Mapping%20Article.pdf.

Case study 5-3, will show how to use cross-group collaboration, strategic leadership, and leadership across organizational boundaries, all much-needed skills in complex collaborative arrangements to recover from failure.

It is critical to properly deal with the human factor when recovering your solution implementation from failure. You do this by providing the participants with psychological safety, which means creating a safe environment that enables candid feedback without the fear of retribution.

CASE STUDY 5-3: SOUL SEARCHING TO RESCUE THE ORIGINAL PURPOSE

In the chapter 2 case studies, we talked about Faith Diaz's experience as young executive with Cloud4All, Inc., a global technology corporation, where she had been working with entrepreneurs for many years. Throughout the chapter, we showed how Faith structured her options for a recommended solution to the need of creating a startup fund for emerging markets. She had to enlist key stakeholders—like government officials, startups, and fund managers—and together they were able to create and implement the fund envisioned by Faith. Unfortunately, several months down the road, the fund's original purpose, goals, and estimate results were off-track. Faith's recommended solution seemed to be the best at the time of approval, but its implementation was going south very quickly.

Now, while she watched the mid-summer sunset through a dusty window, Faith tried to figure out the best way to rebuild stakeholder trust, match their expectations, and ensure a common purpose was reestablished. She had a good idea of what she needed to do, but with so much to accomplish in such a short timeframe, Faith struggled with the prioritization of the several tasks ahead of her.

This happens sometimes, even with solutions that were correctly created, approved, and implemented. In Faith's case, she decided to lead a workshop so that she could identify the best course of action to course-correct the emerging markets fund under implementation. She waited for the meeting participants to arrive, reflecting on several issues that had surfaced along the way—spoiling stakeholder trust, slowing down the implementation process, and leading to key personnel leaving the program. Moreover, Faith had agreed to push at least ten companies through the startup acceleration funnel she was given twelve months to do and, at this pace, this would not happen.

When the fund was publicly announced, the stakeholders felt everyone had a common purpose. The partnership environment was conducive to collaboration where the feeling of psychological safety allowed information sharing with each other to occur freely and in a transparent way. People feel psychologically safe when they are able to voice their concerns and offer feedback without fearing retribution or being ridiculed. With resources in place and the first start-up batch going through the planned activities, Faith's project was initially considered a huge success, especially by the entrepreneurs who now had a viable alternative to fund their companies' growth in spite of emerging markets' entrepreneurship funding scarcity.

But trust rapidly deteriorated between the investment partners and start-up companies due to emerging markets' still-unproven innovation regulations, recurring changes, and outdated labor laws. This last factor led to what became the major source of distrust among the involved parties: the addition of an investor's protection clause in the contracts were a source of tension with the start-ups. In some emerging markets' legal systems, even if a verdict was not final yet, labor disputes can trigger the preemptive freezing of an investment partner's personal assets, which could be set aside for future "worker's compensation." With that, to ensure proper investor protection, investment contracts became very complex. Start-up entrepreneurs are not usually familiar with their country's investment laws and perceive the protection clause as draconian, creating distrust and resentment between partners. Affective conflicts replaced the initial positive cognitive conflicts that led to the fund's creation.

Another issue that surfaced was the ten-year investment cycle required by the international public investment regulatory authorities. This was such a long-term commitment for an investment structure that it is still considered a bet in emerging markets, and this caused anxiety with unclear wins and a lack of short-term ways to measure success. Recurring changes in regulations and labor laws were not well-communicated to all parties, especially to the start-ups, causing missed deadlines and respective penalties. To mitigate risks, investors required extra layers of controls to guarantee that they would recover at least the same amount they invested. This led to the creation of a web of controls over controls, becoming a burden to the start-ups and fund managers. Again, neither the start-ups nor the fund managers and investors were fully aware of how the emerging markets' regulatory environment worked, and the conflicting information generated distrust among partners. The initial excitement about the fund's success, pumped up by a media frenzy, led to a forced group consensus to move on. The start-ups did not feel they had an inducing environment leading to psychological safety and resented the increasingly fast pace to decide and move ahead, causing conflicts along the way.

Now Faith slowly walked back and forth on the patio outside the conference room as she recapped the series of critical decisions that had been made in the last six months, and visualized the challenges she needed to overcome with the group today.

In the workshop, Faith explored the following topics and issues with her guests:

- stakeholder engagement, authorizing environment, and framing challenges as opportunities

- the balancing of technical problems (picking a location for the fund) with adaptive leadership issues (introducing heat sometimes, lowering the temperature further ahead)

- the careful balancing of short-term stakeholder needs with the solution's long-term goals, and

- the positive impact of delivering small wins, regrouping when challenges come up, and providing a safe environment for stakeholder venting.

Faith was successful in her workshop, and able to recover her stakeholders' trust. This happened because she was able to speak to the following critical themes:

- Stakeholder engagement: Faith brought all of them together to solve the problem, instead of trying to do it by herself. Also, she revisited and matched their motivations while focusing on a common goal. She used stakeholder mapping, identified objections and motivations, and defined actions to address these.

- Collaboration analysis: Faith tackled the challenges that came up a few months after the fund kicked off by asking herself: "How can the collaboration mitigate existing issues and improve trust among stakeholders?" The Five Dimensions

Assessment table (figure 5-5) summarizes the collaboration analysis and respective actions to bridge over gaps.

DIMENSION	SPECIFIC ISSUES	IDEAS FOR OVERCOMING
Governance • Are rules in place for decision-making? • Is it clear who gets to decide what issues? • Formal or informal?	• Rules in place, but recurring changes causing conflicting information • Start-ups feeling their feedback not heard • Mostly informal	• Elect neutral third-party to help install governance model • Create feedback loop for start-ups • Ensure psychological safety is created
Administration • Is it clear how to move to action? • Who is responsible for coordination? How is information disseminated? • Formal/ informal?	• Lack of trusted party to decide when to move ahead • Reactive most of the time • Formality through contracts leading to distrust	• Elect neutral third-party to help trusted model to manage changes • Create active information sharing process • Drive regular checkpoint meetings with all stakeholders to mitigate the existing conflicting information challenges
Autonomy • Are we meeting the self-interest of the partners?	• Start-ups do not understand investment regulations and feel kept out of the decision-making loop • Investors seeking protection (labor laws)	• Recover our initial common purpose using the same neutral party as a mediator • Reset expectations and reconnect with each stakeholder's aspirations
Mutuality • Is there enough interdependence among partners (recognition that none of us can solve this by ourselves)?	• Start-ups blame other stakeholders for their own lack of understanding of regulations • Investors try to solve trust issues through contractual protection clauses	• Reconnect to initial purpose with mediator's help • Actively share information and provide with a feedback process
Trust • History of trust or distrust? • Building small wins to build trust?	• Initial high level of trust • Current distrust exacerbated by protection clauses	• Use neutral third-party, small-wins, and back-channeling to rebuild trust • Create psychological safety with feedback loop

Fig. 5-5. Five Dimensions Assessment Worksheet. (Adapted by Melissa M. Stone from Ann Marie Thompson and James L. Perry.)[22]

---

22 Ann Marie Thompson and James L. Perry, "Collaborative Process: Inside the Black Box," *Public Administration Review*, supplement to vol. 66 (2006): 20-32.

The elements below were part of the actual solution applied by Faith following the workshop with stakeholders:

- Faith hired a neutral third party, a consultant, to mediate unsolved issues, fostering psychological safety through third-party mediation. This ensured that a trusted environment was rebuilt among stakeholders that have provided the necessary psychological safety to allow candid feedback.

- Faith used the same mediator to help her stakeholders to reset expectations and reconnect with each other's aspirations to recover the collaboration's initial common purpose.

- After recommitting to a common purpose and rebuilding trust, the group agreed upon a structured, active information-sharing process to be sure that any further changes in regulations, laws, and deadlines were communicated to everyone in a timely manner.

- Faith and the consultant identified opportunities to measure and communicate progress—small wins—along the way, encouraging the group to keep working hard on the long-term goals, something known as the "trust-building loop."

- Back-channeling to avoid confrontation, Faith used a neutral third-party consultant to reach out to dissatisfied stakeholders one-on-one. This helped to control the level of affective conflict and keep the group within beneficial cognitive conflict.

While recalling these issues and how she had addressed them, Faith saw Matthew Cousteau—the consultant she hired as mediator—arrive. He was going to play a fundamental role as mediator in the solution implementation. Faith felt confident that such neutral party would help disarm the participants' skepticism, provide a safe environment for a productive debate, and clear each stakeholder's concerns. In this way, her solution would not only be course-corrected, but even improved with regard to its initial version because of the planned feedback loop. Faith learned from this experience that failure, when well addressed, could be beneficial and make any solution implementation stronger and more sustainable.

CHALLENGE 5-4: CREATE A FEEDBACK LOOP AND SECURE SUSTAINABILITY

Earlier in this chapter, we discussed the organizational lifecycle and its changes after your solution is implemented. When these changes occur, the validity of your solution might be questioned. After all, your stakeholder map may have changed, the organization might have faced a merge or a significant modification in its structure and mission, and resources initially available may have been trimmed out to reflect the altered environment. In extreme cases, the initial solution you designed might not make sense anymore, sometimes because the initial problem has morphed into something else or simply does not exist anymore. Additionally, you have learned about solution failure and recovery, with a special focus on people. All of these items are critical for solution sustainability over time.

Let's cover a different angle of sustaining your implemented solution: when your solution seems to be stable. In this case, Solution Designers tend to just relax and miss the writing on the wall.

Changes might be happening, sometimes slowly, other times concealed beneath the calm waters. How can you ensure that you will spot the signs of change and potential instability? One recommendation is to keep an eye on the intermediate results of your solution (outcomes), while measuring the short-term results (outputs) of it. To increase your solution's sustainability, you must carry out a regular evaluation of its impact (long-term goals). Because of the nature of the solution implementation phase, when Program Managers are focused on ensuring tasks are executed and results are delivered, Solution Designers might stick to only measuring outputs, and in some cases outcomes, but rarely measure the attainment of the original goals for the solution being implemented.

Seasoned Solution Designers know they need to keep an eye on the long term, designing ways to evaluate whether the solution being implemented is delivering on the promises made to the original stakeholders.

As a result of this short-term monitoring and long-term evaluation, you should be able to spot early signs of significant deviations to the original goals for your solution. Below you can find a more detailed description of each of these terms and how they correlate to one another.[23]

- Inputs
  - □ Resources applied in the project to generate deliverables through tasks that are carried out

- Activities
  - □ Actions taken within the project used to implement the solution and measured routinely by the project team

- Outputs

---

23   Harry P. Hatry, "Measuring Program Outcomes: A Practical Approach," United Way of America's Task Force on Impact, 1996: 24.

□ Products or services delivered—short-term results, measured by assessing whether the project is providing the products/services it is expected to provide

- Outcomes
  □ Changes in knowledge, skills, and behaviors driven by the implemented solution—intermediate results which are compounded to accrue to the solution's long-term goals

- Goals

  □ Long-term impact on the organization's mission, accruing up to its vision—transformative changes in attitudes, skills, and behaviors

Figure 5-6 displays an example of a generic organization.

INPUTS ➡	ACTIVITIES ➡	OUTPUTS ➡	OUTCOMES ➡	GOALS
Resources	Actions	Products/ Services	Intermediate	Long-term
Funding	Training	Hours taught	Polished skills	Career growth, bench leadership, end-customer satisfaction
Teleconfer- ence hours	Escalation/ Support	Number of escalated items	Higher productivity	Customer satisfaction levels driving retention

Fig. 5-6. Logic Model correlating activities, outputs, outcomes, and goals. (Adapted from Harry P. Hatry.)[24]

Another mistake made even by the most experienced Solution Designers is measuring outputs and outcomes as well as evaluating goals without an end in sight. The only reason you should measure

---

24 Harry P. Hatry, "Measuring Program Outcomes: A Practical Approach," United Way of America's Task Force on Impact, (1996): 24.. http://www. indiana.edu/~jlpweb/papers/Collaboration%20Processes_Inside%20the%20 Black%20Box_Thomson%20&%20Perry_PAR_2006%20Supplement.pdf

anything is to ensure that you use the results to create a feedback loop into the original solution implementation process. For this loop to work, you will need to start all over again with the I.D.E.A.S. cycle, comparing the results you found to the original information you had when you designed your solution. By doing this, you will increase the sustainability levels of your implemented solution.

Look at the complete Solution-Design Cycle in figure 5-7, with the checkpoint "sustain" at the end.

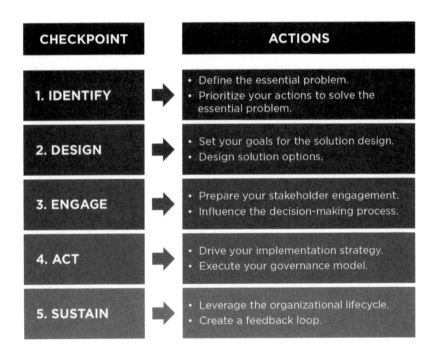

CHECKPOINT	ACTIONS
1. IDENTIFY	• Define the essential problem. • Prioritize your actions to solve the essential problem.
2. DESIGN	• Set your goals for the solution design. • Design solution options.
3. ENGAGE	• Prepare your stakeholder engagement. • Influence the decision-making process.
4. ACT	• Drive your implementation strategy. • Execute your governance model.
5. SUSTAIN	• Leverage the organizational lifecycle. • Create a feedback loop.

Fig. 5-7. I.D.E.A.S. framework for Solution-Design.

Case study 5-4 provides a real-world scenario on how to create this feedback loop. In it, the envisioned solution had just been implemented, the project team had held a great public celebration, and all stakeholders were beaming with satisfaction. Then, over the weekend, the sky fell. The CEO—a key stakeholder and the decision-maker for this solution implementation—abruptly left due to political differences with the board of shareholders. Now what?

CASE STUDY 5-4: LONG LIVE THE NEW KING. IS YOUR SOLUTION DOOMED?

Ray Jones felt like he was walking on air the morning he celebrated his one-year anniversary in his job as Chief Security Officer (CSO) and Vice President of Corporate Security. He had just received the first annual report with the results of his flagship program to raise end-user security awareness. Glancing at the report in his hands, he realized that most metrics showed a positive trend in his departmental scorecard, proving that his team was on the right track to deliver on the commitments made to the company one year previously.

NichePackages, Inc., a thirty-year-old niche packaging company, operated in three continents, with roughly twenty thousand employees and three thousand third parties (vendors, contractors, and other service providers). As Ray rejoiced at the results, he recalled his first day in the job, when the CEO called a meeting to introduce him to his Senior Leadership Team (SLT). His mission could not have been made more clear: the CEO opened the meeting stating that Ray had been hired to develop an End-User Security Awareness Program so that the company could reduce the number of security breach incidents. The tipping point had happened eighteen months prior to that day. A complete marketing memo describing a unique line of business to be launched in three months ended up on major media outlets. With that information spread across the world, the company's competition had seen NichePackages's competitive advantage vanish overnight. They were faster, and launched a similar line of business two weeks earlier than NichePackages, Inc. Millions of dollars in primary research, prototyping, and focus group testing were thrown out the window.

Sure, Ray's company could still try and differentiate themselves from the competition by playing with price and added features. But the damage was done; the competition was seen as innovative, and NichePackages, Inc., was left just a follower trying to "copy" the market leader.

While recalling those stressful moments that triggered his hiring, Ray prepared to deliver the good news to the CEO and his SLT. That was when the phone rang and the sky appeared to fall. It was the Chief Operations Officer's (COO) office calling to postpone the meeting to the end of the week. This was not the issue, after all Ray had other presentations moved to other dates. It was the reason for the meeting's date change that was the issue: the CEO of NichePackages had abruptly resigned the evening before due to political clashes with the board of directors. Staring at the sky getting darker through his window, Ray wondered how his main sponsor's sudden departure would impact his awareness program implementation.

Later that week, Ray was called to present to the board of directors and the SLT in a joint-meeting scheduled to review all programs directly sponsored by the CEO's office. Ray started his presentation by proudly sharing his program's annual report and its almost completely positive scorecard (see figure 5-8).

METRICS	ANNUAL GOAL	YEAR 1 RESULTS	
Outreach			
1. New employees	1,000	835	▲
2. Current employees (baseline 12 months ago)	19,000	18,988	●
3. Vendors, contractors, other providers	3,000	2,966	▲
Feedback			
4. Newsletter click-though	18,000	17,903	●
5. Incident reporting	500	1,412	●
Training sessions			
6. In person	4,000	4,023	●
7. Online	19,000	18,969	▲
Events			
8. On-site clean-desk	6	6	●

● Goal Met   ▲ Attention   ◆ Goal Not Met

Fig. 5-8. End User Security Awareness Program—scorecard, year one.

Ray could feel the environment become heavy in the initial silence, which was quickly followed by rapid-fire questioning by the SLT.

What does "almost completely positive" actually mean? What are your corrective actions to move unmet metrics to completion? What is the *impact* of the activities showing here? Why were the recent leakages not captured here? Even more so: Why they were not avoided? Shouldn't you measure *behavior change* instead of measuring the *number of training sessions*? What is the *cost of reducing incidents* versus the *cost of the program*? Do you measure your program's results against any connection with the business? How should the shareholder's added value be captured? And what is the impact on stock price? Are there any connections to the governance, risk management, and compliance initiative?

Ray could not answer most of these incisive questions. The COO, also playing the role of acting CEO, came to his rescue, saying the points in question were taken, and promising the attendees that Ray would come back in four weeks with all the answers in hand. With that, Ray stopped his presentation before it even took off. He left the room and went back to his office thinking about his now-failed celebration with senior management.

He had four weeks to figure out why he did not have answers for the incisive questions he got a few minutes ago. Where should he start? Maybe it was time to call someone who had enough experience with this kind of situation—his peer, the Chief Information Officer (CIO). Alix Hope, who had referred him for this job, was his former client turned long-time friend. He called and scheduled a meeting with her next day.

After sharing with Alix both the presentation as well as his meeting's experience, Alix reclined on her chair across from him, smiled, and said, "It's about separating monitoring and evaluation." Then she started explaining to him how she used to break down any program or initiative that was longer than two business quarters. She shared tables, graphics, and slides, all correlating short and long-term goals for any implemented solution.

She showed him a couple of slides comparing metrics used for monitoring (short-term) as well as evaluation (long-term), and the difference between both (see figure 5-9).

MONITORING vs. EVALUATION

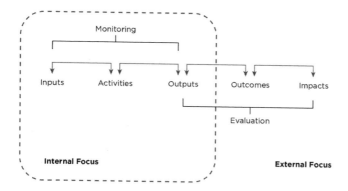

Fig. 5-9. Monitoring and evaluation. (Adapted from Harry P. Hatry, Carolyn K. Lafferty, and Colleen A. Mahoney).[25]

On the one hand, monitoring has an internal focus, targeted at improving the delivery of the outputs. On the other hand, evaluation is externally focused, aimed at proving that the results earlier delivered (outputs) will drive real impacts in the long term (see figure 5-10).

25 Ibid; Carolyn K. Lafferty and Colleen A. Mahoney, "A Framework for Evaluating Comprehensive Community Initiatives," *Sage Journals* 4, no. 1, (2003): 31-44. http://journals.sagepub.com/doi/abs/10.1177/1524839902238289.

PROCESS AND IMPACT EVALUATION

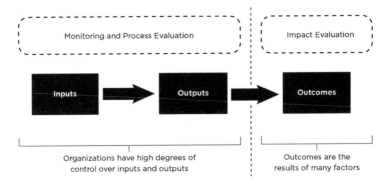

Fig. 5-10: Process and impact evaluation.
(Adpated from Carolyn K. Lafferty and Colleen A. Mahoney.)[26]

Monitoring and process evaluation help the Solution Designer to assess inputs (e.g., funding) against generated outputs. Organizations have high degrees of control here. Impact evaluation helps to assess how outcomes drive real impact in the long term, relating them to the program's goals.

Then, Alix talked about how Ray should use what she called a Logic Model to describe what his End-User Security Awareness Program intended to achieve, a kind of pipeline representing inputs, activities, outputs, outcomes, and goals. The latter one, Alix emphasized, was how Ray could demonstrate the connection of his program to the long-term impact on the organization's mission.

Ray had an "a-ha" moment right in front of Alix. Now he realized why the heat was up in yesterday's meeting with the company's leadership. He had been measuring short-term activities only, making poor or no connection to the program's long-term goals. His departmental scorecard measured only the program's outputs (the products/

---

26   Ibid.

services it was expected to provide), missing any measurement of the outcomes (changes in knowledge, skills, and behaviors driven by it). Moreover, Ray now understood the difference between monitoring and evaluation. The former is used to ensure the program's short-term results (outputs) are on track. The latter should connect the program's long-term results (outcomes and goals).

With that, Ray used the next four weeks to revise his scorecard, create a table with his Logic Model, and define a clear connection between the program and shareholder value creation. Figure 5-11 shows what Ray prepared for his second moment of fame with the board of shareholders and the SLT.

INPUTS ➡	ACTIVITIES ➡	OUTPUTS ➡	OUTCOMES ➡	GOALS ➡
Resources	Actions	Products/ Services	Intermediate	Long-term
Funding	Training	Hours taught	Acquired skills (e.g., better handling of phishing emails by company's members, with 70 percent reduction of Security Breaches by Year 2)	Financial loss reduction by 80 percent by Year 2
Security Help-Desk	Escalation/ Support	Critical concerns escalated by company's members	Higher quality escalation process drives better incident response (e.g., critical security incidents are lowered by 50 percent by the end of Year 2)	Negative impact on company's reputation is recovered by the end of Year 2, with respective recovery on stock price

Fig. 5-11. Process and impact evaluation.

Ray also modified his departmental scorecard to reflect the new vision of connecting short and long-term goals, as shown in figure 5-12.

METRICS	ANNUAL GOAL	YEAR 1 RESULTS	
Output—Training			
1. New employees	1,000	835	▲
2. Current employees (baseline 12 months ago)	19,000	18,988	●
3. Vendors, contractors, other providers	3,000	2,966	▲
Output—Feedback			
4. Newsletter click-though	18,000	17,903	●
5. Increased Incident reporting (behavior)	30 percent higher than baseline	35 percent higher than baseline	●
Outcome—Business Impact			
6. Losses due to security incidents	50 percent lower than baseline	45 percent lower than baseline	▲
7. Customer satisfaction survey	Trust is up 30 percent	Trust is up 46 percent	●
Goal—Reputation Recovery			
8. Annual best worldwide brands report	Top 100	Position 110 (up from 233)	◆

● Goal Met   ▲ Attention   ◆ Goal Not Met

Fig. 5-12. Modified departmental scorecard.

When Ray went back to the boardroom a few weeks later and presented his numbers and new approach to the senior leadership, he was delighted to see that his efforts were appreciated!

Not satisfied with the positive results, Ray took additional steps and decided he would start the Solution-Design cycle all over again. Therefore, he created a feedback loop using the new monitoring and evaluation approach to revisit the originally identified essential problem for which the solution was designed to solve, checking his initial envisioned options, updating his Stakeholder Engagement Map, and revising his implemented solution's goals in light of the new company's reality. After all, with a new CEO to be hired, this was a new business reality that might require adjustments in Ray's program to reflect the new scenario.

This is an excellent way to build a feedback loop into the original solution, from design to implementation. By doing so, Solution Designers can rest assured that their original solutions are sustained over time in spite of organizational changes and people transitions.

Remember, communicate your solution results in a way that your audience can understand and give actionable feedback. Then, go back to the drawing board, input the feedback into the beginning of the Solution-Design process, start over, and revise your implemented solution.

This is the best way to renew stakeholder support, rally leadership behind your recommendations, and sustain your solution's effectiveness.

KEY TIPS FOR CHAPTER FIVE:

1. Acknowledge the organizational lifecycle and leverage it to go through changes.

2. Focus on people to successfully get across the transition zones.

3. Learn from failure to improve your Solution-Design Process.

4. Create a feedback loop and insure sustainability.

APPENDIX --------------------------------------

The following are the authors' top bibliographic references for further reading. More can be found on the authors' website.

1. *The Lean Six Sigma Pocket Toolbook* by Michael L. George, John Maxey, David T. Rowlands, and Marc Price is a guide for users of Lean Six Sigma. It blends various tools and concepts, providing expert advice on how to determine which tool is best for different purposes.

2. *Smart Choices: A Practical Guide to Making Better Life Decisions* by John S. Hammond, Ralph L. Keeney, and Howard Raiffa is a classic, covering one of the best roadmaps for making better and more impactful decisions with a step-by-step, divide-and-conquer approach for decision-making.

3. The Committee of Sponsoring Organizations of the Treadway Commission (COSO, https://www.coso.org) is the report from a joint initiative of five private sector organizations (in financial, accounting, and auditing fields)

dedicated to providing thoughtful leadership through the development of frameworks and guidance on enterprise risk management, internal control, and fraud deterrence.

4. *Influence: The Psychology of Persuasion* by R. B. Cialdini, revised in 2007 is the layman's version of his persuasion book, in which Cialdini explains the psychology of why people say "yes"—and how to apply these understandings.

5. *Influence, Science, and Practice*, also by Cialdini, identifies the main techniques used by persuaders. An experimental social psychologist, Cialdini discusses what he calls the "psychology of compliance," and guides the reader through several real-world scenarios to help us understand why people make decisions to acquire something they are offered (e.g., a recommendation).

6. *Kiss, Bow, or Shake Hands* by Terri Morrison and Wayne Conaway is considered to be one of the most comprehensive references of its kind. This book is a complete guide to international business protocol, covering over sixty country profiles.

7. *Influencer: The Power to Change Anything* by Kerry Patterson et al. covers how to use the authors' Influencer Change Model to leverage the six sources of influence and make change inevitable.

8. *Managing Transitions* by William Bridges describes a model that is helpful to prepare the organization's leadership to address the inherent issues of each phase of the organizational lifecycle, dealing with the present while keeping an eye on the future.

9. *Leadership on the Line: Staying Alive through the Dangers of Leading* by Martin Linsky and Ronald Heifetz delves into the idea that leading requires taking risks that can jeopardize your career and your personal life. This book shows how it is possible to make a difference without getting "taken out" or pushed aside.

10. *Authentic Negotiating: Clarity, Detachment, and Equilibrium* by Corey Kupfer is an Amazon bestselling book that exposes the core of negotiation success and challenges you to do the tough internal work required to become a great and truly authentic negotiator.

11. *Change by Design: How Design Thinking Transforms Organizations and Inspires Innovation Hardcover* by Tim Brown is a great starting point for Solution Designers and how they can apply design thinking principles—the collaborative process by which the designer's sensibilities and methods are employed to match people's needs not only with what is technically feasible and a viable business strategy.

12. *Complete Collection of Project Management Statistics*, written by Emily Bonnie in 2015 for Wrike.com's project management blog, offers statistics, infographics, and a plethora of resources for project management professionals.

13. *Pulse of Profession* is a global survey of project management practitioners put out annually by the Project Management Institute. *Pulse* charts the major trends for project management now and in the future, featuring original market research that reports feedback and insights from

project, program, and portfolio managers, along with an analysis of third-party data.

14. *Adapt: Why Success Always Starts with Failure* by Tim Harford presents a new and inspiring approach to solving the most pressing problems in our lives. Harford argues that today's challenges simply cannot be tackled with ready-made solutions and expert opinions; the world has become far too unpredictable and profoundly complex. Instead, we must adapt—improvise rather than plan, work from the bottom up rather than the top down, and take baby steps rather than great leaps forward.

A Special Offer
from
ForbesBooks

Other publications bring you business news. Subscribing to *Forbes* magazine brings you business knowledge and inspiration you can use to make your mark.

- Insights into important business, financial and social trends
- Profiles of companies and people transforming the business world
- Analysis of game-changing sectors like energy, technology and health care
- Strategies of high-performing entrepreneurs

Your future is in our pages.

To see your discount and subscribe go to Forbesmagazine.com/bookoffer.

Forbes